MEMOIRS OF AN AMERICAN JEWISH SOLDIER

From the Heartland of America

to the Frontline of the Third Reich

To Jeff

By *Bud Sabetay*

Robert [*Bud*] Sabetay

Requests to the publisher for permission or sales should be addressed to:
Sabetay Publishing, Inc.
PO Box 263
Littleton, CO 80160-0263
(303) 757-7100
www.sabetaypublishing.com.

Library of Congress Cataloging-in-Publication Data:

Sabetay, Robert 1924-
Memoirs of an American Jewish Soldier/ Robert Sabetay
Sabetay Publishing, Inc. [2013] 163 pages : illustrations, facsimiles, portraits, maps ; 24
cm; First Edition October 2013
2013916864 | ISBN 978-0-9840713-6-4
Sabetay, Robert, 1924. | United States. Army. Field Artillery Battalion, 773rd. | World War,
1939-1945--Participation, Jewish. | World War, 1939-1945--Personal narratives,
American. | World War, 1939-1945--Personal narratives, Jewish. | Jewish soldiers--United
States--Biography.
D769.34 773rd.S33 2013   ocn880294403
https://lccn.loc.gov/2013916864

10 9 8

DEDICATION

I dedicate this book to the memory of my beloved wife Betty, my son David, my daughter Bonnie, her husband, Dr. Kerry Burte and my three grandchildren: Evan Sabetay, Amy Burte and Alex Burte. I also wish to remember Lieutenant Reams, Lieutenant Maxwell Ivey, and Private Silk without whom there would be less of a story. To all veterans of America's wars, whether dead or alive, I salute you.

CONTENTS

PREFACE

What a surprise it was for me to be a part of the freeing of humanity in World War ll. Through every move, from one division to another: it all appeared as though it were predestined for me. No real harm ever came to me. There were 18 close calls that I distinctly remember; and then there were other incidents that I vaguely remember.

The story of my journey through France, Germany, Belgium, Luxembourg, and Czechoslovakia was full of exciting experiences. I fought in many places from the center of Europe, to south of Germany, and then onto the northern Ardennes, which is where we did our part to win the Battle of the Bulge. I was on the front lines of the Battle of the Bulge for 52 continuous days. We were proud to be under the leadership of General George S. Patton otherwise known as "Old Blood and Guts."

After the signing of the surrender of Germany, I found myself in the Army of Occupation. Many of the incidents that happened to me during that period were also unforgettable. To this day, I remember those things like they happened yesterday.

After the Battle of the Bulge everything seemed to have a different perspective for me. I had no choice but to grow up fast and make mature decisions quickly.

I am now 88 years old and this is what happened to me. I hope you will enjoy reading and perhaps acquire a little better understanding about what happened during the war.

Robert L. Sabetay

ACKNOWLEDGEMENTS

I thank my son, David; my daughter, Bonnie; and my son-in-law, Kerry, for spurring me on and encouraging me to write this book. Without their help this book would not have been published.

Secondly, I express my grateful appreciation to Maria Buzzi who spent thirteen months editing and researching this historical autobiography.

Thirdly, I would like to thank Caroline Sim who did the first editing for me.

Finally, I would like to thank Mr. Cletus Poser of the Fort Myers Beach Library in Ft. Myers Beach, Florida, and Ms. Diana Parker of the Stow-Munroe Falls Public Library, in Stow, Ohio, for their expertise in the production of this book.

Psalm 3: 1-8

Fear Not
A Psalm of David, when he fled from Absalom his son.

Lord, how many are mine adversaries become!
Many are they that rise up against me.

Many there are that say of my soul:
There is no salvation for him in God.

                                                        Selah

But Thou, O LORD, art a shield about me;
My glory, and the lifter up of my head.
With my voice I call unto the LORD.
And He answereth me out of His holy mountain.

                                                        Selah

I lay me down, and I sleep;
I awake, for the LORD sustaineth me.
I am not afraid of ten thousands of people,
That have set themselves against me round about.

Arise, O LORD; save me. O my God;
For Thou has smitten all mine enemies upon the cheek,
Thou hast broken the teeth of the wicked.

Salvation belongeth unto the LORD;
Thy blessing be upon Thy People.

                                                        Selah

A reading from the Holy Scriptures, pp 312-313
Prepared for use of Jewish Personnel of the Army of the United States
United States Government Printing Office, Washington, D.C.: 1942

A PRE-EMPTIVE STRIKE

We were eating breakfast and listening to the radio on that Sunday morning of December 7th, 1941. The broadcaster broke into the regularly-scheduled program to announce that Pearl Harbor had been bombed by the Japanese. His voice had such a sense of urgency in it that my parents were absolutely flabbergasted. I was 16 at the time and remember pondering what this would mean for my near future. America was now officially at war. I knew sooner or later that I would end up in the army. It was just a matter of a couple of years before I could be drafted, so I made the best of the rest of my high school experience. I wanted to date girls, go to dances, and have a normal social life, so

President Roosevelt declares war

consequently that is just what I did for two years. I had lots of odd jobs as a kid to make spending money. One of the jobs was as a newspaper carrier for the Akron Beacon Journal Newspaper. I had 99 houses on my beat and one of my customers had a real honest-to-goodness 35mm film strip of the Japanese strike on Pearl Harbor. He was kind enough to show it to me one day. The thought of going to the war was always in the back of my thoughts but I never let it give me a feeling of dread.

Money was a definite commodity that I needed. I graduated in January and immediately went out looking for a job. Just about anyone in Akron, Ohio could get a job at one of the rubber companies because all U.S. tires were made in Akron.

I applied for a job at Goodyear Tire and Rubber Co. and at B.F. Goodrich Co. I was accepted for employment at Goodrich and worked there from February until May, 1943. My job was to remove the forms from inside the fuel cells that were put into the Army's airplanes wings. Goodrich was rubberizing the cells so they would not explode when a bullet hit them. I was putting out three of them an hour, which made it 24 in an eight-hour shift. This amount of work made the union really angry. I was working too fast. One of the union bosses came up to me and threatened me, but not with my life. He told me to only put out one an hour. I tried to reason with him that a war was on and that our soldiers needed these planes. He didn't care. I told the factory representative who, in turn, told me that I needed to follow the union policy. He took me off the line and gave me an overseer's job. I was no longer in the union. I actually got a promotion. I made $1.25 an hour, but with overtime, I was able to bring home $80 a week.

At this time, I was dating an absolutely beautiful girl by the name of Jean Powell. She was so beautiful that even if I were walking in downtown Akron with her, she would still attract wolf whistles. Jean ended up working at Goodyear making and inspecting fuselages for airplanes. Everyone in the U.S. was involved in the war effort. She was a true "Rosie the Riveter!"

Now I was torn between enlisting in the U.S. Armed Forces and being drafted. The fifth month after graduating from Buchtel High School, the decision was made for me by the U.S. Government. On May 12, 1943, I was duly inducted into the Army.

Rosie the Riveter

I reported to the armory which was in downtown Akron, Ohio on High Street. There were hundreds of men there. They separated us into several groups and we were all given a battery of tests. One of the tests was a urinalysis. Some of the fellows could not come up with their own urine so several men donated theirs. A physical

2

exam was finally given by a physician and we again were separated into groups. This time there were two groups: a large one and a small one. I assumed that I had failed because I was put into the smaller group. I was surprised to find out this was the group that passed. I remember wondering to myself if the donated urine had something to do with the poor results of the larger group.

My dream was to go into the Army Air Corp and become a pilot. I wanted it so badly that I could taste it. As a youngster, building model airplanes was my favorite pastime. Now, I thought, was my chance. I dreamt that one day I would be behind the stick of an airplane. One more hurdle remained: I needed to pass a psychological oral exam. The interviewer was a young psychologist, who was obviously fresh out of college. He struck me as a cocky young man who was impressed with his own importance. I, on the other hand, was a little nervous. I wanted to do everything correctly so that I would get into the Air Corp.

In the course of the interview, I stuttered slightly. This was rather strange for me because I had never stuttered in my life. The interview ended rather abruptly and I asked the psychologist how I did. "You stuttered." He said curtly. "What does that have to do with it?" I said. "In a combat situation, you will fall apart," he replied. Unfortunately or fortunately, his word was final. I wondered how he could be so sure of me. I was very self-assured and his assessment of me proved to be wrong. I never froze in combat. Subsequent events would prove that. Choices of the other arms of the U.S. forces were then offered to me. I chose the Army.

I had never feared the draft because I wanted to serve my country. During the years preceding the war there were rumors as to what Hitler was up to in Germany; but no one really knew for sure. I'm not talking about his takeover of country after country but his planned extermination of the Jews. If the hierarchy of our government knew about this, they sure were keeping it a secret. But as a Jew myself, I wanted to help my fellow Jews. Before December 7, 1941, President Roosevelt had promised America that he would not get us into the war in Europe. He actually won his fourth election by promising no war. Little did we know what was coming our way when Japan attacked us.

History tells us that General Eisenhower suggested to the Joint Chiefs and the President that we needed to put our efforts into Europe first.

PREPARATION

It was a beautiful spring day that morning in May of 1943 in Akron, Ohio. The sun was shining and every tree and bush was in bloom. I really had no idea of what to expect next as a private in the Army. A good attitude would prove very valuable to me, since I was to experience disappointment and hardships as a daily routine. Hundreds of us were loaded onto a train which was heading to Fort Hayes in Columbus, Ohio. We were on the train for the hundred mile trek down to Columbus. We had a good time trying to impress each other with our story telling. Upon arrival, we were all assigned into a different barracks. A corporal immediately showed us how to make our bunks perfectly and so tightly that one could bounce a half dollar off of it. This did not work for me because my mattress sagged in the middle.

Picture of Bud after Basic Training

The morning started with breakfast and then we were outfitted with our new army clothes. Measurements were taken and we then walked down an aisle to pick up our clothing and equipment. When I put on the combat boots, I was instructed to pick up two pails of sand. The holding of this heavy sand changed my 12AA size to an 11B. Evidently the heavy weight with the extra gravity pulled my toes apart and shortened my foot. That was quite a revelation to me.

Next were the injections. We were lined up like cattle going to slaughter, and given injections of all kinds in both arms. The tetanus shot hurt the worse. It made me feel as though I had been kicked by a mule.

After many and various orientations, my group was assigned to the 773rd Field Artillery. We would be going to Camp Bowie in Brownwood, Texas, located in the middle of the state. The old train made up of Pullman cars was filled with the troops. The cooks were assigned to freight cars where they would prepare our meals. After three days on that train, we were very glad to finally get off.

We were then loaded onto trucks which took us to Camp Bowie. After disembarking, we were lined up to answer roll call, and then assigned to our barracks. The barracks were austere wooden buildings with wooden floors. The beds were lined up against the walls with an aisle down the center. The sergeant's room was at the end of that aisle. There was an assembly area at the end of the rows of barracks and a latrine located close by. The latrine was very utilitarian, as was the mess hall. All the buildings looked alike, except the kitchen. It was situated at one end of the mess hall and had a wide entrance to the mess hall building.

I thought about the difference between my barracks existence and my home, but I had no time to reminisce about things. Psychologically speaking, I now know that all the discipline was done to toughen us up. We would be facing a formidable enemy - whether it was the Germans or the Japanese. I was young and impressionable and everything still stands out in my mind, down to the smallest detail.

On the first day the bugle call playing over the loud speaker woke us up at 6:00 a.m. We washed, dressed, and fell into place for reveille. Of course there were calisthenics. Then and only then was breakfast served. Instruction now began in earnest about cleanliness and neatness. We were taught how to hang our uniforms, pack our foot locker, fold our socks, and arrange everything neatly. The barracks were to be kept clean at all times. We were briefed on rank etiquette, whom to salute and when.

On the second day, I was given a rifle and put on guard duty outside of our barracks. Any person found outside of the barracks after Taps played was to be challenged and identified. As I was patrolling the perimeter of the barracks, I spotted a fellow in his underwear headed for the latrine. Immediately, in a loud voice, I shouted, "Halt! Who goes there?" Holding my rifle at the ready, he assured me that he was on a nature call. For the next two hours, I challenged lots of men amid cursing and complaining. This guard duty would prove to be very valuable to me when I was in Europe a year later.

The army's basic training was designed to make us a cohesive unit. We were to learn that there is always power in a 'united front.' This of course was the army's goal and they were quite good at accomplishing it. I would learn that my buddies were the most important people in the field of battle or the line of fire. We were drilled and drilled in cadence counting, "Hut, two, three, four. To the rear column left, shoulder arms left, shoulder arms right, shoulder arms! Present arms! Parade rest!" At the end of what seemed to be a short period of time, our unit looked fantastic for any parade. The discipline of marching went on day after day. I began to become aware of our cohesiveness and bonding.

The time for inspection had finally arrived. Everyone was busying themselves with cleaning, mopping and washing windows. Anything visible to the naked eye was cleaned and spit shined. A lieutenant, donned with white gloves calmly headed to each foot locker looking for dust. Our hopes and expectations were awfully high because passing the inspection would be rewarded with a pass into town. We stood at attention looking straight ahead, not moving one muscle. The lieutenant stopped just short of my bunk and reached up to the overhead rafters. He took his white glove and ran it over those rafters which no one had thought of cleaning. Of course, black dirt came rushing at our eyes like a sudden wind had blown through the building. We were deeply disappointed that we had failed because we had exerted ourselves so much. And no pass.

DISCOVERING ARTILLERY

At reveille the next morning we were assigned to various units of the field artillery. The majority was assigned to field artillery batteries, which were a group of men who handled three field artillery weapons. Some were assigned to a motor pool and some were assigned to the radio section. I was assigned to the wire section. This job involved running telephone wire behind a ¾-ton Dodge weapons carrier. A large reel of wire mounted on the back of the truck played out along the ground. My job was to tie down the wire to different objects such as logs, stones, and other heavy debris. The wires linked each of the three batteries to headquarters. This was very important for our guns and equipment which would be used for a barrage of fire power on our enemy.

Basic Training proceeded with a vengeance! After all, we were being trained for major battles. Reveille, bivouacs, and maneuvers were an important part of our training. How well we did was important because our very lives were at stake. I kept a very positive attitude during this period. As hard as all of this was, my one biggest annoyance was K.P. I hated K. P. (otherwise known as Kitchen Police) with a passion. The peeling of potatoes and cleaning up seemed to be endless and thankless. A typical day with KP started at 4 a.m. and lasted until 10:00 p.m. By then all I could think of was falling into my bed and sleeping like a log. Sleep was the only thing I had on my mind after a stressful day in the kitchen.

Word came to us that we were to pass the General's inspection on the parade grounds. Rows upon rows of soldiers were lined up in the hot Texas sun. From the corner of my eye, I noticed one of our soldiers collapse from the ranks. First there was only the one who fell forward. Then there were two. Then there were several. Thank the Lord, I continued to stand in that hot sun, as the other soldiers were picked up by the medics and hauled off to the hospital for heat prostration.

Our first bivouac was in the panhandle of Texas and it was focused on artillery firing. The huge artillery guns were set up: communications with headquarters was tied into us; and forward observers were in place. The target was an old junk car, which was nine miles away from us. Our guns were fired at maximum range after I finished tying in all of them with my wire. A 4.5 shell was rammed into place. Then, a cloth-covered gun powder charge was loaded. A smaller charge was also loaded behind the initial charge. The breach was slammed shut. The Gunnery Sergeant was in charge. We all waited with baited breath as he shouted, "Fire!" A lanyard was pulled. A large shrill explosive noise rented the air. The gun carriage jumped back on its trail and the shell was on its way. I watched the firing of the big gun from several feet back. It hurled out of the muzzle. The shells fell short of the target! Our next volley landed fifty yards over the target. The forward observer called in the adjustments and the next volley landed on the target and split the old junker in two. Later, a large diamond T-wrecker with twin booms picked up the wreckage and hauled it away. Eventually everything was packed up and arrayed behind 6 X 6 GMC trucks. The term "6 X 6" stood for four dual driving wheels that were in the rear of the truck and two driving wheels in the front. The artillery pieces were towed by a yoke formed by the trails of the guns fastened to the back of the trucks. Two rows of wooden bench seats were folded down in the back of the trucks and our crew was able to ride with our new best friends, our big guns! We were grateful that a canvas covering protected us from the Texas heat.

After returning to our barracks one evening, soldiers took a matter into their own hands. A scrawny looking fellow who hadn't bathed for eleven days because he hated showers, was unceremoniously grabbed and dragged to the showers. The body odor was so horrible that none of us could stand it anymore. A brown Proctor and Gamble soap was applied to both the soldier and his uniform. Amid much hollering, a stiff brush did the trick and this poor fellow came out of the situation looking rather pink.

This same fellow was in our barracks one day when he should not have been there. After questioning him as to why he was there, he mumbled something under his breath and quickly retreated through the nearest door. It was not long after this

9

episode that he was dismissed under a Section Eight ruling. A Section Eight ruling is given for mental instability.

Our next bit of training included the firing range. We soon found out that even though we hit our target, the judges would not give us credit for it. They would wave a pole that told us that we had missed it completely. This was called Maggie's Drawers. When it was my turn to be the judge of the bull's eye, I had my fun with the other shooters. That evening when I undressed myself, I was black and blue from my shoulder to my waist. It was from the heavy Lee Enfield rifle hitting my shoulder over and over again. At the end of rifle training, I was relieved and surprised that I had qualified as a sharpshooter. This training in rifles would prove to be invaluable to me when I was marching through Belgium, Luxemburg, and Germany.

Extra training in calisthenics was given to us along with running and fast walking in full gear in the 120 degree semi-desert of the Texas Panhandle. The dust made a white coating on our skin and our own perspiration evaporated quickly in the arid atmosphere. We slept under the stars and quickly found out what the night sky can look like without the interference of city lights. Rattlesnakes were present and liked to cuddle up at night to a nice warm body. Equally torturous was spreading your blanket over a ground cactus.

My body had been conditioned and toned by basic training with calisthenics and running. We were to have a calisthenics run off. I was paired with a cook who was one of the slowest men at camp. We were to do 50 pushups, then run 100 yards one way, then turn around and run back 100 yards. I was constantly waiting for this poor fellow who was woefully out of shape because of his kitchen duties. He collapsed at the end of the second hundred yards and was on the ground in great distress. His face was drained of blood and he turned snow white. His breathing was so labored that he was gasping for every breath. Fortunately, he recovered sufficiently after ten minutes and was able to put one foot in front of the other.

That evening I was assigned to guard duty. About two in the morning I became very nauseated and started shivering. I completed my guard duty even though I was feeling very ill. When I reported for sick call that morning, I found out that 600 men were sick that night. The reason I waited until morning to report to sick call was that I did not want anyone to accuse me of being a softie. The medical staff attributed the sickness to soap that was left in the kettles at the KP. Improper rinsing of the kettles caused all of this unnecessary trouble.

There wasn't much mercy being passed around by the army doctors. There was one event where I was treated rather roughly by a physician. It was a pimple on my left forearm that became infected. My forearm was quite red and swollen. The Doctor told me that there was nothing wrong with my arm and to ask the cook for a kettle to soak it in. I thought to myself, "Yeah, sure. The cook will throw me out if I dare ask him for a pot." So I decided to stick my arm in the sink at the latrine and run hot water from the faucet over it. It did the trick and the thing finally broke open with a clear fluid pouring out of it.

One thing about the doctors in the army was that they did not fool around with toothaches. I had one heck of a one and was sent to the dentist immediately. The dentist was a burly, extra tall man who probably weighed about 260 pounds. He told me, "You have four wisdom teeth coming in and you don't have any room for them." Then he told me, "I have to pull them." He immediately gave me a couple of shots of Novocain and did the extractions. I was not allowed to lie down after the procedure so I went directly back on duty after I left the dental clinic.

SOME NICE GIRLS

U.S.O. dances were regularly held on the base. Busloads of girls were brought in and, of course, I met one. She was a pert little brunette. She agreed to see me only if I would go to her Baptist Church with her on the following Sunday. I did. I must say that it was quite an experience for me. The preacher shouted at the people with a hell-fire and brimstone message.

She then took me to her home where I met the rest of her family. The afternoon was a sunny one and her brother had a horse, which was quite spirited. Her father asked, "Would you like to ride him?" I should have known that this was a set up. I had very little riding experience but answered, "Sure." No sooner had I mounted the horse and grabbed hold of the reins, when the horse exploded into a dead heat run. Before I had time to rein him in, he ran into an orchard with low lying branches which scraped over my back. I proceeded to throw the reins down, grabbed a hold of the horse's neck, and hung on for dear life. He made a U-turn in the middle of the orchard and ran full blast all the way back to the barn and into the stall pinning me between the stall and the roof. They slowly backed the horse out of the stall and I gingerly dismounted him, as they held the horse amid peals of laughter. Although this was done in good humor, I felt totally embarrassed.

We were given three day passes for a 50 mile radius. My cousin, Evelyn Beckerman, lived in Dallas and invited me for a stay with her and her husband, Mike. There was only one problem with the invitation; Dallas was 200 miles from Camp Bowie. I thought if I kept my nose clean and stayed out of trouble that everything would be fine. After my cousin picked me up at the Dallas bus station we drove to her home. Evelyn's home was a brick ranch on a quiet street in an upscale neighborhood. They had two great cars. One was a 1941 Cadillac Torpedo two-door sedan and the other was a 1939 Ford two door-sedan. Mike owned an auto parts business in downtown Dallas.

After I was settled into the spare bedroom, Evelyn made sure that I had access to the 1939 Ford. She introduced me to several Jewish girls, who I asked out on dates. One girl asked me to accompany her on a date with a visiting sergeant in his convertible. I was flattered but he was not, which I could understand. She evidently did not trust and care for him all that much and wanted me along as a buffer.

Another girl, who was a Southern Methodist University student, used to make my heart skip a beat when I would speak to her on the telephone! "Buddy, Honey," she drawled in that sweetie sweet southern voice. "When are y'all cumin to see me?" Upon hearing that sexy southern drawl, my heart definitely skipped a beat.

My last day there, Mike introduced me to a young lady who came from a well-to-do family. We dined at the Baker Hotel in downtown Dallas where a well-known band was playing Glenn Miller music. An ugly incident marred the evening. My date was spurred by a Cavalry lieutenant, who was wearing spurred boots. She didn't tell me about the incident until we sat down. By this time the lieutenant was gone and there was nothing I could do to make things right. I was very angry at what this guy did to my date. And, I think he did it because I was just a private who had a good-looking girl on my arm. He probably could not come up with a good reason as to how I had gotten into such a swanky place.

The dance floor was filled with well-groomed men and women dressed in formal attire. All of a sudden the movie star, Robert Taylor, walked into the room with his mother. They made a grand entrance: with him in his well- tailored officer's uniform and her in a beautiful evening gown. He was definitely a cut above the normal handsome man, with his jet black wavy hair and perfectly chiseled features. The women in the room went gaga over him. What an end to a perfectly wonderful evening. I will never forget it.

The evening was over and I had to return to Camp Bowie. Mike took my date home and dropped me off at the bus station. The bus that pulled up was a tractor with a trailing bus. It was about 11 p.m. when we departed. For the first two hours the ride was uneventful. Then the bus slowed to a standstill on a two lane road in the middle of a prairie. The bus was loaded with soldiers on the way back to camp. We all spilled out of the bus wondering how we were going to get back to the base. A truck came along, stopped, and four of us climbed up on the open trailer part. We were prepared to ride back to camp until we discovered that it was a sheep truck, full of bleating sheep, complete with sheep dung. We then saw a car coming down the road so we all jumped off the truck and hailed the car down.

To our utter amazement the car stopped. There were already two soldiers in the front seat. Three of the guys climbed into the back seat and I got in front between the two other soldiers. This was a heck of a lot better than the sheep truck. The driver drove for about an hour and proceeded to stop at a roadside diner for five minutes. He must have been very sleepy because after about five minutes he asked me if I could drive. I told him that I could and he said, "Fine, you drive, but keep it down and don't go over sixty miles per hour or you will overdrive the headlights." As I drove along, the moonlight swept the two lane black top road ahead. I noticed a stopped car parked broadside across both lanes. I made a split-second decision to veer left on to the prairie, past the back of the car and then went right back onto the road. I don't know why but I thought there might be hijackers in that car. I did not want to put all of us in peril by stopping. To this day I think about that incident and feel that I made the right decision. It was five in the morning before we pulled into Camp Bowie!

I was dropped off just in time to make it into the barracks, change my clothes, and fall out for reveille. After reveille a soldier complained to Sergeant Shaheen about me. "Why is Sabetay allowed to go 200 miles on a 50-mile pass?" Sergeant Shaheen responded, "He shows up for reveille!"

Someone in our group decided that a brilliant training idea was to have a free-for-all. Even though none of us had any offensive or defensive training, we found ourselves in the middle of a brawl. 'What a stupid way to train troops,' I thought. I approached the milling circle of men with apprehension, not knowing what the outcome would be. I barely got into the fringe of the circle when suddenly a pair of rigid arched fingers filled my vision. A numbing sensation struck my eyes as the fingers attempted to gouge my eyes out. My vision went white. Not being able to see, I stumbled out of the free-for-all and attempted to regain my sight. After ten minutes of seeing white, my vision slowly returned. I could hardly believe that this was a planned endeavor because none of us was prepared for any of this. A lot of us were hurt.

14

Setting up guns and laying wire was our next training challenge. A captain did not think we were proficient enough in this area. One day he was riding in a scout car and seemed to be really shaken up. A sergeant told me that the scout car hit a tree stump and ripped the guts out from under the car! I made the mistake of asking him if he was OK. He ended up giving me back a glare that could have killed. Instantly I learned my lesson regarding the boundaries of propriety. Another time we were on a forced march with an ambulance following us in the event that any of our troops became ill. The captain fell out after we were about half way there, and had to use the services of the medics. His nickname was Captain One Nut because it was rumored that he only had one testicle. At that time, I did not foresee that this captain would end up being a real adversary for me! My assessment of him, along with the other guys in our unit, was that he was rather weak both physically and psychologically. Later on in Europe, he certainly proved himself to be a bigot.

Despite being raised a Jew, I really had not yet experienced any anti-Semitism. I grew up in a Christian neighborhood and no one ever bothered us for being Jewish or for having a different religion from them. I was in the latrine one morning when a 35-year old blonde soldier expressed his dislike for Jews to me. His attack on me seemed so violently provoking that I could have gotten into a knock down drag out fight right then and there. However, I made a quick decision to ignore him. I knew that in the 1930's there were German Bunds[1] in the U.S. Then, because of the war with Germany, those groups were outlawed. Where was this numbskull coming from? I chalked it up to prejudice and ignorance. I thought that he might have been a member of the Ku Klux Klan. He attacked my core value and I definitely saw red! However, I kept my cool and made an allegory of it in my mind that compared him to a person who just did not like potatoes. My personality was laid back enough so that I was able to keep my composure most of the time.

---

[1] A German Bund was a political organization in America which was filled with Nazi sympathizers.

There was a prison camp in Camp Bowie where German POW's were kept. Most of the prisoners were from Rommel's African Campaign. Basically they were a clean bunch, well fed, and cared for. They didn't look too terribly unhappy. Seeing them got me to wondering how American POW's were being treated behind German enemy lines. It would not be too much longer before I would find out for myself. Camp Bowie was not only home to the Field Artillery but to other army units such as the Fourth Armored Tank Battalion. We had heard that this group was overly trained. Our paths crossed much later in Germany. They exposed us to phosgene gas and deadly mustard gas so that we would know how to handle it and what to do if it came upon us on the battle fields. We entered a small wooden building and then we were gassed. Drills with gas masks would prove valuable. To me, the mustard gas smelled like newly-mowed hay.

Furloughs were available alphabetically and I always waited hopefully for my name to pop up quickly but it never did. I started getting suspicious after some men had gotten two furloughs. I was visibly upset. When the visiting Inspector General came to hear complaints, I really wanted to tell him that I felt that I was being denied my furlough which would have been a nice 14-16 days but I did not want to complain, feeling that they might interpret it as squealing. At this same time there was a drive for Army Air Corps recruits. I applied and took the tests at the camp hospital. One fellow who preceded me on the tests sat down next to me. I asked him what was on the test. He told me there was a maze and one had to follow a path through the maze. The information he gave me was helpful and I passed the physical and the mental tests. I did not hear from the Air Corp right away because the Lieutenant Colonel delayed my furlough and sent me on maneuvers in Louisiana, completely ignoring what was sitting on his desk. All of these mishaps and delays in furlough got me wondering if they were mistakes or were they being done on purpose because of my ethnic background.

The U.S. of A. was a different place in the 1940's than it is now. This was long before the era of Dr. Martin Luther King Jr. and the civil rights movement. There was segregation in all of the armed forces during that period of history.

Word came down that we were to go to Louisiana for maneuvers. The trucks were loaded and we headed for Louisiana. It was late in the season and the weather had turned cold. Frost and mud occupied the fields. Pup tents were pitched and, as it turned out, I became the odd man out. These tents were made to house two people but I had no partner to share with. I pitched my tent over some very tall grass. The next morning I woke up absolutely freezing, with my teeth chattering and I was chilled to the bone. I pulled my fatigues over my woolens. I put my army coat over that and then my raincoat over everything and I was still shivering. The odd part of this was that I should not have been there. Orders had come down for me to report to Sheppard Field which was an Air Corp base in Texas. These orders were received the day we left for the Louisiana maneuvers. The Lieutenant Colonel knew this and sent me on these maneuvers anyway, hiding the fact that my furlough was also on his desk. He purposefully delayed my long-awaited furlough and ignored my orders to report to Sheppard Field. Boy, what a set-up. I was experiencing injustice first-hand on a small scale but just a smidgen of the injustice Jews in Germany were going through. A lieutenant and driver picked me up in a jeep and hustled me to Leesville, Louisiana. Riding in an open jeep with temperatures in the 20's was not conducive to getting warm. It was now quite obvious that I had the flu.

Leesville, Louisiana was like a wide open frontier town with hundreds of American soldiers milling around it. I was quartered in a two-story building walk-up with another soldier. Across the hall were two buxom, rough-looking girls who were probably ladies of the night. We both decided to stay very clear of those two ladies. On the street that night we could see where soldiers had been robbed, black-jacked, and left to be picked up. We could hear honky-tonk music blaring from nightclubs. Drunken soldiers sprawled against the walls of buildings. The place looked like a frontier town from a cowboy movie.

The next morning I headed for a barber shop where I proceeded to get a shampoo, haircut, and a shave. Later on that day I was transported back to Camp Bowie where I was sent to the base hospital with a severe case of the flu. Three days later I felt somewhat better, was released and sent to Sheppard Field, five miles from Wichita Falls, Texas. They had me listed as AWOL. This took a bit of explaining but the staff checked my story about the delay, the maneuvers, the flu, and decided that I was, indeed, telling them the truth.

SHEPPARD FIELD

After being quartered in a barracks, I was put through all types of tests. One of the tests consisted of holding a stylus on a small quarter-size disc that was rotating on a phonograph turntable. Another was a hearing test. They seated me in a quiet dark room where I had to look at a cubicle. A ticking watch was brought near my ears then moved away. I had to listen until I could not hear anymore. I passed this test quite well. Another test consisted of maintaining a miniature plane mounted on springs on an even keel. There were two pedals inside that required me to depress one, and then the other to control it. I would depress one and the plane fell to one side. Keeping it on an even keel seemed unlikely until I discovered that if I rapidly depressed the pedals back and forth I could keep it on some semblance of balance. Even though this method worked, it was not the best way. I found out from the sergeant that there was a possibility of breaking the machine. Another test was to look at pictures of airplanes coming at you while you were inside a bomber. You had to take notice as to where they were: twelve o'clock high, or six o'clock low, or anything in between.

Later on I was interviewed by a psychologist at some length. A colleague walked in the room and interrupted us by telling the psychologist that his young daughter was suffering from a sinus infection. They both turned to me and asked me what I thought. Sensing a trap, I did not comment at all. I knew then that they were on to my history of sinus trouble. Finally and gently, the psychologist told me that I could not fly because of my sinus trouble. However, the good news was that I had scored very high on gears and mechanics and I would be transferred to Amarillo, Texas for B-29 propeller school. I probably owe some of this success to the building of Gilbert Erector Sets when I was a child. That experience taught me about different gear ratios.

Twelve hundred soldiers were fed in the mess halls at one time. A request came over the speaker one day asking the men to quit taking the silverware home. They were missing 1200 pieces of silverware just about every day because the newlywed men were attempting to set up housekeeping with the government-issued silverware. I was overwhelmed by the variety of food that was served in the Air Corp. I tried to eat a little of everything but still could not eat all the variety. I ended up going from 145 pounds to 165 in no time at all.

I eventually was assigned to KP duty. Remembering my old KP duties at the 773rd Field Artillery set me up for a worrisome time of feeding 1200 hungry men. This turned out to be an unfounded fear because they had potato peeling machines that did all the work. I was assigned this duty at night. At midnight, the sergeant in charge informed us, "We will take a break!" The break consisted of frying up prime steaks and eating them. This was one of the tastiest and easiest KP duties I ever drew. It was a pleasure to work that night shift.

Sheppard Field was a very exciting air base. B-17s were taking off while other planes were landing. Hearing the roar of engines was exciting for me. It was like a dream come true. When I was a youngster, I built and managed to fly model airplanes. I remember a Ryan low wing monoplane with rubber bands being a little underpowered. Launching and flying the plane in a vacant field next to my house always brought on a wave of euphoria as my planes became airborne. Now reality had taken the place of fantasy for me.

Guard duty consisted of guarding a pump house on the fringe of the flight line. Some of the guys were assigned to cockpits of fighter planes. I complained to the sergeant of the guard, saying that I also wanted to sit in the cockpits. "What are you complaining about?" he asked. "You are staying in a warm pump house while those guys are freezing their butts off in a plane on a cold, windswept runway."

AMARILLO FIELD

The orders came transferring me to Amarillo Field in the Texas Panhandle. I was, as usual, assigned to a barracks, but there wasn't much to do as I was waiting to be assigned to B-29 propeller school. A nice bunch of fellows were also assigned to the barracks. We soon found common ground in our personal circumstances and experiences.

One day we all got a pass to town. Amarillo, Texas was only six miles from the air field. The only thing that would delay me was that I was assigned to window washing duty. The First Sergeant assigned me to wash hundreds of 8X10 glass windows in the supply room. There were approximately 24 lights per opening. After much grumbling that it would take forever, my two buddies stepped in and said, "We are not going to town unless you come with us." The Sergeant pointed out that if we all tackled the task together it would not take us long. A half hour later we were all finished.

We had a long walk to the bus station so we tried to hitch a ride. A Ford convertible passed by us and I recognized the driver as the film star Donald O'Connor in an Air Corp uniform. Evidently, he did not care to pick us up. That was one song and dance movie star that lost my respect that day. We finally caught a bus to town and found a dance hall that had booths around the perimeter of the dance floor. The county we were in was dry so we ended up buying our own mixes for our drinks. A couple of girls danced with my two buddies and joined us at our booth. One girl I remember well was a tall nice looking girl name Pat.

Pat had a little too much to drink and it affected her in a very peculiar way. She became a crying drunk. No matter how funny our conversation was, Pat would end up crying and rather profusely at times. We still managed to have a wonderful time that night and the memory of those times always stayed in my mind. They were good and fun times for me. Not much to do at Amarillo was the norm for me as I kept waiting for my orders. Windy Amarillo! Perhaps that is why the army built an airfield there. There were lots of high ranking important people in

Amarillo, some with diplomatic intentions and some who would eventually end up in the State Department.

One of the men acquired an emergency leave from the Red Cross to go home on a furlough. This prompted me to think that I may be able to get a furlough finally, especially after I was cheated out of mine from the 773rd Field Artillery. I still believe in my heart that this action against me was because of anti-Semitism. In my next letter home I wrote, "I understand that Mother is not feeling well. Do you suppose that you could get in touch with the Red Cross and I could get an emergency furlough home?" Not long after I wrote that letter, I was called into the sergeant's office. He inquired if I knew anything about my mother being ill. "I knew she was not feeling well," I answered. Since all letters going out were censored, I knew that he was suspicious. However, I was granted a 14-day emergency furlough home. Finally!!!

FURLOUGH

The next problem was how to get home. It was wintertime and there were some flights in a B-25 going north from Amarillo. However, I couldn't seem to catch one. The next best thing was a train. The first part of the trip home was shared by a fellow cadet. He proceeded to tell me how he seduced and conquered women. He would woo them and then become engaged to them. After becoming engaged he would talk them into marital pleasures and then suddenly disappear. He asked me what I thought of his methods. I did not comment except to say that I thought it to be highly unusual. To myself, I thought, 'What a rat!'

Flooding had washed out a bridge, so the train had to take a detour through the state of Georgia. This is where I met up with a card shark who tried to convince me to play poker with him. I repeatedly told him that I did not play cards with strangers, so he kept on showing me one card trick after another. He admitted, "I'm traveling to a carnival. I know 1001 card tricks." He smiled and then entertained me for the rest of the trip home.

Arriving back in Akron was a very happy occasion for me. The subterfuge worked and Mom looked better than ever to me. Mom, Dad, my twin sister Reva, and my younger sister Elaine, all greeted me warmly. Dad had a C Gas Ration Sticker for his 1938 Olds as he was a partner in the F&S Auto Wrecking business. This made it easier for me to get around Akron for dating and having fun. I did not have to worry about transportation. Everything from sugar to gasoline was rationed in the U.S. during the war and I felt very lucky to have the gas to put in the car. Also, some gas was siphoned for me from the lacerated cars in the wrecking yard.

My sister, Reva, arranged a few dates for me while I was home. It felt so good just to date and not have to return to the base. One girl was especially beautiful with dark hair and a willowy build. Chewing gum was hard to get back then, but the minute I walked into a store in downtown Akron with her, it was given to me. Because I was in uniform, I was respected and given a little extra kindness for my service to our nation. All of America was behind us, and everyone was involved in the war in one way or another.

But, I had made up my mind that I was not going to get serious about any girl before going overseas. I did not want some sweet young lady worrying her heart out about me. Before I knew it my 14 days were up and I was back to the Army Air Corp.

CAMP HOOD

Upon arriving at Amarillo Field, I learned I had missed being shipped to Fresno, California. The bad news was that I was now slated to return to my old outfit, the 773rd Field Artillery. Another soldier and I were given our army papers and travel orders. This fellow soldier was an extremely good-looking, tall guy with black wavy hair. His looks were rugged and he sure had a personality to match it. We hit it off quite well and ended up taking a bus to Lubbock, Texas, where we were supposed to catch another bus to camp. He said to me, "Bud, do you realize we have all of our army records and we could even go home or get lost." Lubbock looked like a very nice town so we just decided to stay a few days and enjoy ourselves. We found a hotel room, cleaned up, and went out on the town.

On the third day an MP stopped us and quickly asked us for our traveling papers. When he noticed that we were three days late he asked why. I explained that when we arrived in Lubbock it was so late that we missed our connection. That night we decided we had better catch the next bus out.

When we got to Camp Bowie we learned that our outfit had shipped out a few days before. They assigned us to Post Casual where we were to stay until our outfit sent for us. A friend of mine named Mark knew all the angles for getting on and off the base. With his knowledge, we were able to get in and out of town with no trouble at all. The camp bus took us into town. We met a couple of nice girls who were fairly nice looking and made a date with them for the next night. We took the camp bus back into town. We then hitched a ride on a tractor trailer truck with a sixteen year old driver. He drove us another sixty miles to the town where the girls lived. We had a great time laughing, telling stories, and just relaxing. Later that evening, we hitched another ride back into Brownwood. We missed our eleven o'clock curfew and were in violation of the rule. Trying not to be noticed in the town, we shadowed our way to a taxi cab station and hired a cab to take us back to camp. The cab sailed right through the gate without being challenged. We did this little fete one more time with the same great results.

Finally my orders came down for me to join my outfit between North and South Camp Hood. Camp Hood, which is now named Fort Hood, is 60 miles north of Austin, Texas. Upon arriving I was assigned to a four-man cottage type building. It had a wooden floor, sideboards, and screens from the sideboards to the beginning of the ceiling, with a canvas top. The mess hall was some distance away and was a long one-story building with wooden tables and benches. I was assigned K.P. duty on a permanent basis, even though there was no reason for this.

One of the brief respites I enjoyed was skinny-dipping in a creek. We had a wonderful southern gentleman by the name of Lieutenant Bean who was the man in charge. He was one of the classiest men I had ever met. I remember him as being about 5 feet 10 inches tall with fine features and straw-colored straight hair. He recognized all of us as having value, including myself. One of his jobs was to be our camp censor. He was ordered to read our outgoing mail. Remember, 'loose lips sink ships!' That is why we had to have our mail read by him. I had the deepest admiration for

Troops getting off busses

him because his character was sterling and his action toward all of us was respectful.

Finally an exciting day had arrived for me. My mother was coming to visit me at South Camp Hood. The time came for mess hall. I was about five yards behind the last man to enter the mess hall when Captain McCloud saw me and said,

"You're confined to quarters!" "Why," I asked. "Because you're late for mess!" There was no reason for Captain McCloud to act this nasty way to me because I was not late for mess hall. The orders for my leave had to come to his desk, so he already knew about my mother's visit. This was my second little altercation with Captain McCloud.

After eating I headed for the Charge of Quarters office. I figured that the charge soldier on duty would not know what just went on with Captain McCloud, so I signed out because I had a pass for town. Since I was only a private, I reasoned that I had nothing to lose. I arrived at South Camp Hood just a short while later. Upon checking the guesthouse, I discovered my mother was not there. She had cancelled her trip and was not coming. There was no way to find these kinds of things out in the 1940's. Communication was fairly primitive as compared with today's cell phones and e-mails. I decided to go to the PX and once there, I wandered around for a while. I ran into a fellow soldier who told me that the MP's were looking for me and that I was in big trouble. There were thousands of soldiers in tan uniforms. How could they find me in this crowd? "We all look alike," I told myself. Early in the evening I caught a bus back to camp. On the bus a fellow soldier again told me that the MP's were looking for me and that I was in a lot of trouble. None of this seemed to bother me because I felt so righteously indignant about the whole situation. I felt that I had been singled out. Upon arriving in camp I checked into the Charge of Quarters building and signed in. The soldier on duty was the same soldier who had checked me out. He threatened me with dire consequences.

Sergeant Shaheen was very unhappy with me because I had put him in a precarious position. I not only took an unauthorized leave but I did not go through the machine gun obstacle course. The next morning the two of us took off for the obstacle course in a jeep. Sergeant Shaheen drove that jeep about seventy miles an hour and we arrived at the camp about half an hour later. I was instructed to crawl under barbed wire, to keep my head and butt down while a fifty caliber machine guns' bullets whistling over my head. After completing the course I was taken back to camp where I was to learn my fate. I was either to be sent to Fresno, California or to Headquarters Battalion. They chose the latter for me.

My job was in the machine gun squad. I definitely did not relish this job. One day I saw a fellow soldier who looked longingly at the machine gun squad. He was in the radio section. Seeing an opportunity to get into the radio section, I asked him if he would like to trade places with me. His eyes lit up. I spoke to a fellow tech sergeant in personnel, who happened to be Jewish, and asked him if he could help me. A few days later a transfer came through for me to be in the radio section. This was a true break for me. The best part of the job was operating a radio in the back of a scout car with my feet propped up. I had a microphone in my hand relaying messages between the front lines to the guns in the rear.

Training continued and we all became proficient at our jobs. We were notified that we were to pack and load our equipment for a train ride north. It was a troop train with many coach cars and a mess car in the middle. For three days we ate, told stories to each other and watched the scenery.

CAMP SHANKS

We finally arrived at Camp Shanks, New York, which was an embarkation camp. After being assigned to a barracks, we were assembled and told that when we went on pass into town we were not permitted to tell anyone where we were stationed. Security was very high and the well-being of the troops was very guarded. The old adage was told to us over and over again, "Loose lips sink ships!"

Another soldier and I headed to New York City, crossing the George Washington Bridge. It was a memorable sight, especially knowing that we were all to ship out soon. That evening we went to a dime-a-dance club. The hall consisted of many girls lined up waiting for someone to ask her to dance. We purchased a roll of dime tickets at a ticket booth. Each dime-

dance lasted exactly one minute. The lady dancers acted like they were very disinterested in us. In a very short time the tickets were gone and we needed to purchase more. At this point we decided to leave. One has to be pretty starved for female companionship to subject oneself to that kind of abuse. My friend had a grand idea. He wanted to go to the top of the Waldorf Astoria where 'Jimmy Dorsey's Band' was playing. We arrived and looked over the menu but decided at those prices all we could afford was a beer. We nursed our beers very slowly and carefully and eventually asked for the bill. The waiter told us, "Someone sitting at the bar has picked up your bill." We conveyed our gratefulness to him, but left soon thereafter. During the War, the general population was extremely kind to servicemen.

I received a letter from my father because he wanted me to know that he was coming to Brooklyn, New York to see me. I had not seen Dad in about a year and was very excited about his visit with me. He stayed with my cousin Sid

Olstein, her husband Joe, and their two kids. I took the subway to meet Dad and was made to feel welcome at their house. Dad looked very well except for his swollen ankles which worried me a little. There was another visitor one day at Sid's who kept inquiring where I was stationed. He certainly was persistent but I would not tell him where I was staying. All I could think about during this inquiry was that assembly where they told us, "Loose lips sink ships." Dad and I mostly talked small talk about my sisters, gas rationing, his job at the wrecking company, and the like. My twin sister was working at O'Neil's Department store in downtown Akron as a photography clerk and my other sister was only fourteen. We both knew that I was headed overseas and I don't think that Dad wanted to burden me or make me anxious about going. All of us soldiers were all a bit anxious about it with a nagging 'butterflies in the stomach' type of feeling.

My Uncle Reuben, who lived in New Jersey, invited me to dinner with his wife and two children, Bob and Sarah. They in turn introduced me to a pretty girl with a warm smile and a good personality. We went to a small park where we sat on a small bench. We were getting along famously with kisses and small talk when we were rudely interrupted by a beat policeman. That was a rather abrupt ending for a guy going overseas and needing a nice diversion with a pretty girl.

I knew that it could not be long now before we would be leaving for overseas. The army seemed to have sympathy for us because we were given free rein on our passes. A rather pronounced melancholy feeling came over me because I knew just enough to make me anxious. Three of us shared one pass into New York City. We met three girls from New Jersey and proceeded to Coney Island where we rode the rides and had lots of carnival type-fun.

I proceeded to go to a fortune teller who turned out to be a very attractive gypsy woman. Our knees were almost touching as she sat directly across from me. She took my right palm and read it. She said that I had a very long life line and that I would survive the war unscathed. It was time to read my left palm where she foresaw that I would have two children, a boy and a girl. Every time that I subsequently found myself in a tight spot I kept holding onto what she had said and

I felt that I would be alright. I just needed to be reassured from someone that I was coming back alive. I also do have two children; a boy and a girl.

Rumors that we would embark any day were everywhere. My last visit to New York was to the Stage Door Canteen. Upon entering, I was taken by the hand of a young pretty woman, rather tall with beautiful features and about in her mid-twenties. She sensed my melancholy mood and decided to cheer me up as much as she could. We talked about life, developing character, and positive things. I greatly appreciated her concern and left there feeling much better.

OVERSEAS

Our day of embarkation arrived and we packed up all of our gear and got ready to board. The ship was named the H.M.S. Tamara, a British ship weighing around 12,000 tons. It was built in 1922 and was the first ship that was all welded. It was originally a ship that carried meat and had huge hooks on its walls for this. I was assigned to the forward well. There was a huge open hold with tier upon tier of bunk beds. Several hundred of us were quartered there with a single light bulb hanging in the center to illuminate the hold. My bunk was the third one up with a huge ventilation fan over my head. Soon tug boats arrived to pull us out into the harbor. The throbbing of engines was heard everywhere. We sailed that afternoon in June of 1944 and the next day we joined a convoy of hundreds of ships that were spread out over the horizon, as far as the eye could see. Our speed was twelve knots; however, it still made us all feel as though we were sitting ducks. One knot is equal to 1.8 mph. Life jackets were issued to all of us. They even came with a red light for us to use in dire circumstances. What the nautical staff did not tell us was that we only would survive in the North Atlantic for a few minutes before dying of hypothermia. Plus, what vessels would ever stop to pick up survivors after being torpedoed by German submarines? All of this was going through our heads and our hearts. We were growing up pretty fast for a bunch of teenagers and young men in their twenties. That night we watched the bow make ripples, turning a regular dark ocean into a luminous wonder with sea creatures and other living organisms. What a beautiful thing to behold in the middle of a voyage to fight in a war!

There was one pleasant room on the ship. It was the dining room which had a nice mural painted on the walls amidst several porthole windows which gave a very nice view of the ocean. The tables and benches in this mess hall were anchored to the floor. The food consisted of boiled potatoes, bully beef which was English corned beef, and very doughy bread.

On the third day I became violently seasick so I sought comfort *amidships* (middle of the ship) on the deck. I was told there was only one way to overcome this: Always keep food in your stomach. Since I could not keep any food in my stomach, I took some bread from the kitchen which was practically raw and forced myself to eat a little at a time. Eventually it stayed in my stomach and I stopped throwing up.

Often I would leave my stuffy bunk in the hold below and lie on the deck until 4:00 a.m. when the crew would come on duty to swab down the decks. They would kick me out. Now it was time for me to take a salt water shower. Those wonderful things were given on the forward deck. But after having one which proved to be cold and sticky, I was not in any hurry to return to that.

One evening while watching convoy ships stretching out as far as the eye could see, I saw two destroyer escorts off the port bow. They seemed to be in a big hurry and were dropping depth charges. We thought that there must be a German sub trying to get to us. We never learned what was going on during that little scary episode.

GREAT BRITAIN

The sea was kind to us and we sailed into Liverpool, England two weeks later. As we pulled into the harbor, we saw a sunken ship with its bow sticking about 30 feet into the air. The bow of the great ship had been pockmarked with a thousand shafts of light taking the place of where steel had been. Later we learned that the ship had been an ammunition ship and had been blown up and sunk.

After disembarking the ship, we were loaded onto a train and taken to the very green and picturesque countryside of Wales. I will always remember the ride there because of the great beauty everywhere. We quartered down in a Quonset hut on the grounds of an old great English country house. The showers, in another Quonset hut, were very cold, but at the same time rather invigorating. The great house had the headquarters in it, including radio and communications equipment.

Headquarters settled in and we started training on our equipment. My radio, a 600 set, was to be used on our jeeps. The radio sergeant, a pleasant fellow with fair hair and a nice personality, aligned the set for me. I watched him carefully because I wanted to be able to do this myself the next time around. A fellow soldier warned me not try this on my own, but felt I could be successful. When the sergeant left I tried to tune the set myself and align it in six easy steps - unsuccessfully. When the radio sergeant returned from his short recess he saw that I had taken the initiative and was pleased with me. He then walked me through the steps a second time and I was successful.

It was now time for some passes to town. We loaded ourselves onto two-and-one-half ton trucks. It was a very interesting ride because the roads were narrow with high walls in some of the villages. It seemed as though we were barely going to make it through the narrow mazes, but we did. Most of the Welsh boys were on the continent of Europe or at least fairly far away from Wales, so we advantageously had our pick of the English girls. As soon as we hit the town most of us went off hurriedly looking for female companionship. I hooked up with a rather tall, buxom, blue eyed-blonde, and she wasn't bad looking either. We seemed to hit it off with each other immediately. There wasn't much to do in the town except to eat out at a fish and chips restaurant. Our order arrived when I noticed a couple of gaunt looking pre teenage boys hanging around. One of the boys grabbed a piece of bread right off of our table and ran. I thought to myself, "No wonder the poor kid looked so gaunt. He must be starving to death." It was hard for me to believe that in the heart of England there were people who were starving. I was to later find out that most of Europe was suffering food shortages because of the ravages of the war.

Because we were waiting for our orders for departure to the continent, we basically had nothing to do. We ended up honing our personal skills and pulled a lot of guard duty. We were told to guard an empty field with two brick posts at its entrance. There were two of us on duty when a couple of Welsh girls appeared carrying picnic baskets. "Hi, Yanks,' they hollered. "Want to join us for a picnic?" "Sure," I answered. "But we are on guard duty," answered my colleague. "That's true. You stay at the post and I will talk to the girls over there." He agreed to signal me if anyone came. They had set out their table cloths on the grass about fifty yards away. We could actually see for miles because of our location, consequently, it was pretty safe. Giggling and talking dominated our afternoon with the girls. Had I been caught, I could have been shot for dereliction of duty. Guard duty is taken very seriously in the Army and it is nothing to mess around with.

We got to know the townspeople fairly well. I struck up a conversation with an elderly English gentleman one day about trucks. He said that he preferred American-made trucks because their engines were easier to access to repair. I took his word for it since he was a mechanic. My experience with the British people was a very good one. I think that they were so appreciative of us being there to help them win the battle over Hitler. We could tangibly feel their friendship and warmth. We all knew that it would be just days before we were to go to the French beaches. D-Day had already taken place and we were to be the next wave of soldiers.

LANDING AT NORMANDY

A few weeks had gone by when we received orders to pack up our gear and move to the Eastern seaboard of England. As we were riding along in the trucks, I noticed tons of artillery equipment and a myriad of supplies for mile upon mile. We sat fully armored in battle dress with helmets, weapons and rations. There were long lines of tracked vehicles towing artillery pieces, halftracks, and tanks. There was so much equipment and hardware that it looked as though the island of England would sink from the mere weight of it all! While we were waiting in line to board the ships, we saw what appeared to be a delectable bakery shop. The promise of honest-to-goodness baked goods proved too strong and several of us made our way to the shop. My mouth was watering as I chose the most delicious looking sweet roll. What a surprise it was for me when I took my first bite. The sweet roll had been made without sugar. Sugar was rationed at the time. What a disappointment that was for a soldier ready to embark on what would be the final episode of World War II. Eventually we reached the beach in England and loaded onto a Landing Ship Tank (LST).

I will never forget the sound of that bow door closing as we headed out into the English Channel. This was it! Yes, this was really it! There were ships of every description which were all headed for Normandy. Three-quarters of the way across the Channel a captain took the microphone to give us a pep talk. He appeared to be swaying back and forth and it was not the normal swaying that one would get from the water hitting the boat. He was obviously drunk and we all knew it. "Sabetay!" he shouted with a loud voice. "You're a fuck up!" My thoughts were racing! What had I done to be humiliated like this in front of hundreds of men? "You don't even know how to wear a Mae West jacket!" Just then a stupid soldier deliberately bumped my carbon dioxide cartridge on my Mae West life jacket causing it to inflate. Two navy officers suddenly started struggling with the captain, while trying to seize the microphone from him. They were unsuccessful and he continued to berate me in front of two decks of troops. I wondered why they couldn't get the microphone plug pulled. There was not much I could do because I was so hemmed in by the surrounding troops. We were packed into that LST like a can of sardines.

36

All I could do was stand my ground in my inflated life jacket and wonder what brought all of this on. Could he be violently anti-Semitic? There were waves of it in the army and I had experienced it before. Religious tolerance in the USA was pretty slim pickings in the 40's. There was definitely an undercurrent in the army of anti-Semitism and the worst of it seemed to be learned in West Virginia and other southern states. The history of America certainly points that out. I could not dwell on what had just happened to me as the anticipation and tension of the approaching beach pushed all other thoughts aside.

The ship glided almost to the beach, opened its huge doors and dropped its ramp. We ran off into waist high water. The shock of the water was not as bad as I thought it would be probably because my adrenalin was at its peak. The beach had been partially cleared of a lot of its debris from the battle of Normandy; which made an easier way for tracked vehicles and artillery. All of this stuff had been stored in the bowels of the ship, and they were now making their splashing entrances onto the beaches. We continued past battle debris, worked our way up the beach, and then raced to catch up with the advancing troops.

Normandy was full of hedgerows, which had been secured by our troops. Since our troops had secured these hedgerows, our outfit continued on west of them. Late in the afternoon, we bivouacked in a field near a fence. We were warned that we were near enemy positions and to keep a sharp lookout. Our machine guns were set up in a parameter defense and we prepared to spend the night. It wasn't long after dark that the silence was broken up by a putt-putt noise in the sky that broke the evening quiet. High in the night sky were silver objects, rocket shaped, with short stubby wings and a tail. These turned out to be the V1[2] rocket bombs that were sent from Peenemünde, Germany. Their destination was London, England. The rocket would leave or be launched somewhere very close to us in France: then once it was over London, England an eerie silence would occur just before it hit its targets. British pursuit planes were able to shoot down some of

---

[2] The V1 rocket bomb was the world's first cruise missile. An unmanned gyro guided plane with a predetermined mileage had London set for destruction. It absolutely terrorized the British people and was nicknamed the Doodle Bug.

the V1's but not all of them. The V1 was an extremely swift bomb that was jet-propelled.

Indeed much later that night, stuttering machine gun fire punctuated the stillness and jarred me out of a nice sleep. In the morning we learned what all of the commotion was about. It seemed that a machine gunner thought he had seen movement in the dark and opened fire. I would say he probably had a good case of primary combat jitters. Eventually morning came and revealed a fencepost with neat holes right through the center of it. At least his aim was deadly!

While moving up to a position near the front lines, we crossed a small bridge over a deep creek and pulled into a circular pattern on a flat plain surrounded by some low hills on three sides of us. We had just bedded down for the night when a German Focke-Wulf 190 - a low wing radial engine plane - dived over the bridge and flashed by doing about 350 MPH. Two riflemen on both ends of the bridge opened up fire on the plane; shooting low on the approach, and high as it left. The plane flashed by so fast that four of our 50 caliber machine guns on the back of a halftrack did not even budge an inch. One of our riflemen heard and saw the plane before it got to us. He was fortunate enough to get off a few shots which proved to be sufficient to chase the plane behind a hill. Our stalwart Lieutenant Colonel, who was a very tall man, ran away with a blanket over his head looking like the headless-horseman in the 'Rogues of Sleepy Hollow.' When the story made its rounds, we all had a good laugh at his expense. I must say his past treatment of me made it even more enjoyable for me.

ACTION WITH THE ARTILLERY

We moved out the next morning in pursuit of the advancing troops. The 773rd Field Artillery Battalion settled down in a picturesque valley. Behind us were beautiful hills where our guns were set up. Close-by pine woods with log covered slit trenches abandoned by the fleeing Germans became our camp. That night a droning noise rising and falling heralded the approach of a German recon scout plane. A German Storch affectionately referred to as Bed Check Charlie, paid us a visit on every night we remained in that position.

In order to enhance our slit trenches, pine trees of five inches in diameter were chopped down and put on the trenches for camouflages. Shorter pieces of pine trees were used along with more wood and dirt to really try to hide us.

Later in the evening a few stray rounds of artillery fire from the enemy dropped in on us. But we were not too alarmed. We fired back at a maximum range of ten miles. It was decided that we should move closer to the action. The Lieutenant Colonel had a scout car with two rear view mirrors mounted on the running boards. The Lieutenant Colonel kept looking into his rear view mirrors in utter horror. I went along as his radio operator on this scouting expedition. Another location was picked out. It was a rolling grass hill with a small valley. At the base of the hills we nestled in for what we expected to be a prolonged engagement.

When off duty, some friends and I scouted the area to see what we could find of the enemy. We did find an ME 110 German twin engine bomber crashed on a hill behind us. There were deep holes about six inches in diameter punched into the front at an angle. We also found some unexploded bombs buried deep into the ground. Shattered Plexiglas lay on the ground and I remember picking up a carved piece which I quickly used to repair the crystal on my Bulova watch.

After settling in our new area, my duties as a radio operator in the headquarters company took on a whole different aura. Target ricochets came back on through the radio. We were evidently bombarding the fortified city of Metz. It was very quiet in the headquarters tent, with only the hum of radios, and the whispered plots of artillery officers who were on duty.

Soldier with a radio like mine

One of the other radio officers related a story to me about the infamous Lieutenant Colonel of 773rd Field Artillery. He was in the headquarters tent when he thought that he heard incoming fire. No one else heard a thing. He proceeded to ring up 'Able-Battery' which relayed," No incoming fire." He rang up B and C Batteries which reported no incoming fire. Finally he rang up D Battery which also reported, "No incoming fire." Shortly thereafter the Lieutenant Colonel was removed from command. I did not see him again for some time. He certainly seemed to be a nervous wreck and may have received treatment for this. This was the same Lieutenant Colonel who denied me my furloughs back at Camp Bowie and my orders for the Air Corp. One lesson I learned about bullies was that when confronted they whine, cry, and retreat.

There were all kinds of mishaps that occurred during the war that stand out in my mind. One was that our Taylor Craft observation plane was flying the same path that our shells were passing. I asked a fellow soldier if that was dangerous. He told me that it was not because the pilot flies at a different altitude and away from the shells. Satisfied with his explanation, I continued to watch the Taylor Craft flying overhead. Just then there was a large puff of smoke in the sky and the plane disappeared. Well, I thought to myself, 'So much for explanations!' The only thing that was found after the plane exploded was the pilot's wallet. This was the same pilot who used to give us takeoff and landing airplane rides. He was a real swell guy. I felt so badly about this guy's death.

Another time when I was on duty at headquarters tent I heard a very important conversation on the radio. Our American soldiers were on the roof of the Metz fortifications pouring gasoline down the ventilation shafts and then dropping live hand incendiary grenades down them. The ensuing explosions forced the Germans out and the fort was captured. Metz was a heavily fortified city in Northern France which was a pivotal point during the war. The Nazi's had had control of Metz from 1940 until we assailed it in November of 1944.

Men marching on the outskirts of Metz

Our battalion was on the move again. This time I was riding in the back of a jeep with a bare steel crossbar fixed overhead. The driver was driving at breakneck speed across a very rough field. He hit a rut and catapulted me straight up into the steel bar overhead. My steel helmet struck the bar with such force that it knocked me senseless for a few seconds. I later discovered there was a four-inch dent in the top of my helmet.

The battalion bivouacked that evening and I discovered a new use for my dented helmet. It made a great washing bowl for a long overdue sponge bath. Two of our soldiers returned from an outing in a French farmhouse where they said they had drunk and partied with a French couple. They said they asked lots of questions and, according to them, they gave lots of answers about our outfit. Being curious, I

41

asked them what they told them. "Well, we told them what we do," they answered. It was obvious that they were not thinking clearly and the so-called French couple was really German agents. As far as I know, nothing really bad came from that conversation.

It was time to move on again. The next important event was at the famous Maginot Line, the site of a great battle that had just taken place. The Maginot Line was a line of concrete fortifications, tank obstacles, artillery casements, machine gun post and pillboxes that went on for at least one hundred miles. It was thought by France to be impenetrable. It was constructed between 1930 and 1940 in anticipation of another war. When we arrived on one of the hills, the graves registration was dragging and piling both American and German dead soldiers. A wire was tied to a leg and the bodies were then dragged. Upon reaching the crown of the hill, we could not believe the carnage. Dead bodies were everywhere, frozen in grotesque death poses! Rigor mortis had set in and frozen them in their last actions of fighting. None of us could take a step without careful placement of our feet or we would step on that 'sea of humanity.' One large, very handsome, dead American was frozen in a crouching position as if he was coming out of a foxhole. Another German with the top of his head blown off and his brains exposed was lying off to the side. We, of course, had never been exposed to this kind of carnage. I felt totally numb after my initial shock. It was not long after seeing this that we all sat down to eat. This might sound callous but, it was our only way of surviving. I will never forget that handsome American who was frozen in death!

The Maginot Line

Just below the crest of the hill, there was an entrance to the Maginot Line

Fort. We entered a long tunnel with rooms off to the sides. *Sappers*, special engineers who detect and disarm mines, were busy planting explosives. A radio room with huge glass tubes of all kinds of radio equipment came into view. Two of us secured some large radio tubes and left. The explosives experts urged us out of there because they were ready to blow up the place.

When we returned, the 773rd again pulled out and set up in a field of small rolling hills. At this point, we were still in the French countryside. There was a coniferous forest that ran parallel to us approximately 400 yards away. I was sitting in the back of a jeep waiting for the executive officer to appear. He was to take us out to zero the artillery in when my radio sergeant asked me for the spare transmitter microphone. Just then the Lieutenant Colonel who was previously removed from command showed up. I thought I would never see this guy again. Life is strange. He climbed into the back of the jeep, and sat down beside me. His bony ass hit the microphone jack and bent it. Another executive officer showed up and jumped into the front passenger seat. The Lieutenant Colonel then climbed down and we took off.

Bud with German Artillery Gun

We traveled for about four miles and pulled off into afield to zero the artillery in on some German troops several hundred yards away. I was transmitting coordinates when the microphone went dead. Having no spare, we had to return without zeroing in the guns. Murphy's Law reigned supremely that day.

Things were moving at a rapid pace now. Hitler's much-vaunted troops were retreating into Germany proper. The battalion set up at another location which was very similar to our last location but the main difference was that the fields were more open. A new technology involving searchlights shining on the clouds at dusk and reflecting back to earth was tried. It must have had mixed reviews because I never witnessed it again. Another innovation was the *proximity fuse*. Artillery shells had this fuse in their noses.

As the shell neared its target a radio wave was reflected off it causing the shell to detonate in the air showering enemy personnel with shrapnel. I also witnessed a barrage one night on an enemy town. It was just like fireflies blinking on and off while they lit up the rooftops of houses.

My next and last experience in the 773rd artillery battalion was in a small German town. We were somewhere in Bavaria and I was operating the radio for headquarters. I was in a small house where we set up a radio relay station in a second floor bedroom. We set up a cable from the bedroom down the front of the house to a scout car radio. Relaying messages from the front observation ports to the field batteries from the comfort of a bedroom was my radio sergeant's idea of clear-cut luxury. After the battle of Metz, the German fortification located in France, this duty seemed like a real breeze.

The small town I was in was empty and deserted. Buildings and houses were totally empty. Sporadically, a few artillery shells would land in the town. Of course, the noise made by these shells was very noisy. I stayed at my post and operated the radio on the second floor. One radio operator, whose name I do not recall, ran for the basement and cowered there. He did this every time a shell came in. His nerves fell completely apart by the next day. We were getting bored in this town so we went to every empty house and collected every wall clock and cuckoo clock we could find. We brought them back to our radio room and hung them up on the walls. The symphony at noon and midnight was absolutely glorious.

I was so bored now that a slow-moving rabbit caught my interest. I decided to capture it by hand. The poor thing was nothing but skin and bones and it was shivering to beat the band, so I released it.

A little while later I found some soap to wash my hands. A fellow soldier commented to me that lye soap was probably made from human fat. "What are you talking about?" I asked him. He didn't answer immediately but went on to say, "The Germans have lamp shades made with human skin." I asked him again,

"What are you talking about?" He did not answer me but turned and walked out. He knew I was Jewish and I believe that he was being sensitive to my feelings at that point. We were beginning to hear stories of what Hitler was doing with the human bodies of the Jews, Gypsies, and the mentally or physically disabled and other dissidents who openly disagreed with him.

INFANTRY AND THE BATTLE OF THE BULGE

A communication came down that replacements were needed for the infantry. We were to draw straws to see who would go and who would stay. I drew a straw to stay for three consecutive days. However, I was told that I would be going as a replacement. I was still a private and had not earned a PFC stripe or a good conduct medal. What we did know was that we were part of General Patton's Third Army, and that he was asked by General Eisenhower[3] to help with the Battle

Generals Eisenhower, Patton and Bradley

of the Bulge. They needed foot soldiers and they needed them badly. So, in a matter of three days I went from the artillery to the infantry. It was not called the Battle of the Bulge at that time, but we knew that this was probably the last great

---

[3] Dwight David Eisenhower (Ike) was the 34th President of the United States and was previously a five star general in the army. He was the Supreme Commander of all of the Allied Forces in Europe.

battle of WWII. Rumors were spreading like wildfire that the Nazis were hurting because the Allies were making great gains by taking back Paris, and Rome, and of course Normandy. No one was exempt now.

I gathered my belongings together the night before I was to leave. Before I fell asleep that night, I cried silent tears. In my spirit I knew that this mission was very a very dangerous one. All was on the line for every one of us. The seriousness of it just got to me. I felt a lot better after my cry. When morning arrived I started to say goodbyes to my friends. I told the guy who fell apart at the sound of a few stray shells to keep his chin up. I said goodbye to my radio sergeant who was very kind and considerate to me.

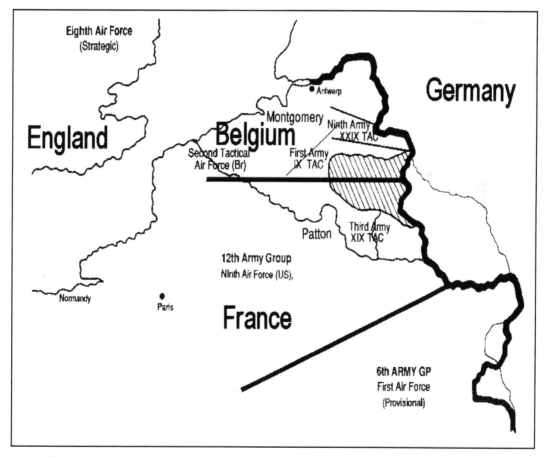

The hatched area indicates where the Germans had <u>bulged</u> through the allied line.

We climbed into the back of a two-and-a-half ton truck along with our duffle bags and were taken back to Metz. Upon arriving in Metz, we heard all kinds of rumors. There was this big push on by the Germans which caused a bulging into our forces line in the Ardennes Forest. This is how Battle of the Bulge got its name. (*A more detailed map is located on Page 70*) We bedded down for the night. In the morning we were outfitted and given M1 rifles. The army personnel taught us how to take them apart and put them back together. They also taught us how to load and fire them. A sergeant from the 95th infantry took us on patrol and taught us some basic infantry tactics. He also taught us how to disperse and present as small of a target as possible, by not bunching up. "When you aim at the enemy, line up his chin on the front site and, squeeze one off," he told us.

Because I had extensive training on the firing line with Lee Enfield rifles and carbines in the artillery, I readily took to the new training. When I was in the Army Air Corp, I also had training on Browning Automatics Rifles, otherwise known as BAR's. One other important thing the sergeant taught us was to never retreat from the enemy's artillery fire, but instead to advance.

Another bit of advice that the sergeant gave us was, "Green troops tend to shuck off equipment along the line of march." We saw gas masks, blankets, overcoats, and other things that get awfully heavy to carry. I could understand firsthand about the overcoats, but not the blankets or the gas masks. We were in Metz for approximately one week when this very important lesson would prove useful for victory and our own salvation.

On the morning of December 23, 1944, we all hopped into six two-and-half-ton trucks. Our duffel bags were tossed in beside us but in my case, my bag was thrown on top of me. My thought at the time was, "Oh well, at least I will keep warm." Later I realized what a mistake I had made thinking that because I couldn't even wiggle my way out from being under it. The other men were piled on top of their bags and they could not move either. I found out that our driver was an African-American soldier, by the name of Ed Hewitt. Here he was from my hometown of Akron, Ohio. To this day he is still living in Akron and I see him every once in a while. His assignment was to drive us to the Ardennes Mountains.

The Ardennes is a region of extensive forests, rolling hills, and ridges named within the Givetian (Devonian) mountain range, primarily in Belgium, Luxembourg, and stretching into France. The Battle of the Bulge was fought here; starting on December 16, 1944, until February 7, 1945. It was one of the bloodiest battles of the war occurring within months of the end of the war. American started with 83,000 troops and increased to 610,000 troops. American casualties were 19,000 killed, 47,500 wounded, and 23,000 troops captured. Germany started with 200,000 and added reinforcements of 100,000. In the end, Germans had 84,834 missing, captured or wounded.

We were off onto a one hundred and eighty mile odyssey to meet the enemy. This ride northward is stuck in my brain to this day because of the lack of conversation and my constant struggle to free myself from the big heavy duffel bag. Everyone had their own personal fears and they did not feel like talking. Besides, it was two days before Christmas. Most of the men had very personal thoughts at that particular time of the year. The cold countryside, snow-covered hills and trees, rolled by as the truck roared northward.

It was late afternoon before the trucks stopped at our destination, an open field with the Ardennes Forest to our left and right. I was assigned to the 90th T.O. Division, which stood for Texas Oklahoma. Roll was called and we formed up and moved out, descending a hill right toward the enemy.

The troops spread out to the left and to the right of a tank destroyer. A captain with his right hand on the back left side of a tank waved the troops forward. I ran full tilt forward with my rifle in my right hand going right toward the tank. A guy to my left said, "I'm going to get that cowardly son of a bitch hiding behind that tank." We all felt that this captain was a coward because he continued to stay behind the tank and not run up in front of the troops to take his proper place. I ran to the front of the tank and hit the ground behind a slight rise in the landscape. There was a lieutenant to my right front who was peering at two Germans with a pair of binoculars about 300 yards front and center of the plain. The lieutenant shouted, "Cease Fire! There is a German medic assisting a wounded man." All up and down the line the word passed and the firing died down. It was absolutely incredible! The German medic faced withering fire from us and still tended his wounded comrade. That was the day that I learned to respect my enemy.

Some thirty yards in front and to the left of me was a GI. I was getting ready to move up to him and so I stuck my left hand into the air when instantly I felt a sting and explosion simultaneously. My left forefinger in my wool glove started to turn crimson red. A German *Panzerfurst* (anti-tank rocket) fell short of the tank ahead and exploded. The G.I. who was thirty yards in front of me was gravely injured. Gingerly, I pulled my glove off. To my relief my finger was still there. It was numb, stinging, bleeding profusely but still there. The bleeding stopped eventually and I was able to move it.

Rumors started flying that there were six-foot German troops holed up with six-foot German girls. Someone probably dreamed this after the heat of the battle that first day. As dusk fell, we bedded down in a mature pine woods for the night. The Germans, who had just been there, left their slit trenches covered partially with pine logs. I shared a slit trench with a guy who had frozen legs from the knees down. All night long incoming Nebelwerfer rockets of twelve round barrages kept coming without a let-up. The explosions among the pine trees sounded like a harp

Men marching at the Battle of the Bulge

with their low deep vibrations of shrapnel twanging off the trees. I asked my new-found bunk mate how he could walk much less run, with frozen feet. He said that he did not feel anything but was able to run. We tried to catch some sleep but with the constant barrage of rockets, nicknamed *screaming meemies*, it was difficult.

About 4:30 in the morning, I blinked awake from a twilight sleep. A quiet creaking, rumbling noise woke me. I recognized the sound of a tank and proceeded to break out into a cold sweat because I knew I was in imminent danger. KAPOW! A sharp loud explosion broke the night quiet. Then I heard clank, clank, clank and nothing more. An hour and a half later we moved out past a huge German Tiger Royal Tank. It was tilted up on the side with the turret pointed toward the ground and the 88 canon nose break was buried in the ground. We moved silently past this monster as if we were trying not to awaken the sleeping giant. Even though this gigantic machine was demised, it was still haunting all of us who looked upon it. The German war machinery was formidable.

Daylight was beginning with the first rays of sun splashing across the plain. I felt hungry and realized that I must eat something. I cut open a K-ration carton and ate a small can of cold beef and pork as we shoved off on a forward attack. We spread out across the plain, running toward the enemy. I had not yet fired a single shot because I hadn't seen any Germans.

At the same time, about fifty yards in front of me and to my left, was a tall and slim American Lieutenant. He kept urging us forward: waving us in the direction that he wanted us to advance. The scary thing concerning this lieutenant was that he had evidently gotten shot and geysers of blood were spurting out from under his arms. Out of the corner of my eye I could see him sink slowly to the ground as I ran past him. He had fallen due to the blood loss. This incident stands out in my mind as if it were yesterday. No one could forget the price he paid for doing the right thing.

An American tank destroyer equipped with a new high velocity 76 mm gun crossed the little rise in the road in front of me. The raised road that the destroyer was on bisected the plain of the land. .The road looked like it was a half of a mile long, but then the rest of it disappeared from my view. I remember that the road went on up a small hill. The tank destroyer raced up the hill, fired twice, and two German tanks were knocked out. When we reached the road, a swarm of incoming artillery shells started screaming in and dropping all around us. It felt like I had died and gone to hell! Moreover, the sheer fire power of the shells was deafening and chaotic. Since the road was raised above the plain about 18 inches, we crawled on the plain, to the left of the road.

A kid by the name of DePasqualle was the acting Corporal. He was now in charge; nevertheless, I kept encouraging him. He was in front of me by a few yards. I kept yelling at him above the roar of the shells," The Germans do not shell their own troops." The plain on both sides of the road was covered with fresh snow. The shells kept coming continuously without a let up. They were exploding on both sides of us. Every time that they exploded they would leave a cone of black cordite far out in front. Now a shell cleared the road, roared over me, and exploded about fifteen feet away. The shrapnel from the shells hurled forward with phenomenal explosions and concussions (shock waves). By all rights I should have been dead.

I was lying face down in the snow with my knapsack on the top of my back. That knapsack had gone up and down in the concussions along with me. There had to be three major concussions that occurred, plus they also drove me deeper into the snow. I picked up my head and started crawling forward. The snow was darkened with black cones of fire every ten feet or so. I kept up my yelling to DePasqualle pushing him ahead. My hands were so cold that I could not fire my rifle if I needed to. I did not realize it at the time but my left forefinger swelled up to twice its size. I believe it was after this battle that I was listed as Missing in Action for about three weeks.

As we neared the top of the hill, we crossed the road and charged upward. I ran across two German soldiers, who could not have been over the ages of thirteen or fourteen. They were cowering against a rocky ledge. They had thrown their weapons away which I saw just a few seconds before discovering them. Gray with imminent death staring them in the face, they were shaking like leaves. I ran past them and hoped that no one who was behind me would shoot them. At that time we were told not to take any prisoners. Later, I heard two shots ring out but I didn't know if it was for them or not. In my heart, I just could not shoot these mere teenagers. Hitler was losing the war at this point and he and his generals knew it. Instead of surrendering they had decided to use young teenagers to replace their heavy losses.

We eventually reached a rocky knoll. It was past a burned up German tank. A G.I. saw me and his eyes got as big as a couple of saucers. He said, "Sabetay! That's not you." "What do you mean?" I said. The G.I. stuttered, "You're dead!' "No I'm not!" I said. "But I saw you get killed!" He yelled unbelievably! "Well, I didn't!" I replied.

We settled down on high ground and tried to dig in. Unfortunately, it was extremely cold and our shovels rang and threw sparks as we tried to dig into the frozen earth. After digging down a few inches it got easier, but then we hit rock.

Finally we took stock of ourselves and settled in. I saw a German about three hundred yards to the left as I looked down the hill that I just had come from. He ducked down behind a giant oak tree. I took careful aim, set my sights for three hundred yards and squeezed one armor piercing bullet off. My M1 rifle would not fire. After that, I sat down, took it apart, and found a slug of ice behind the chamber that was the exact size of an M1 bullet. After cleaning it out I reloaded it and fired several rounds at the base of the tree. I don't know if I got him or not, but I never saw him come out from the other side of the tree.

Another soldier and I were discussing the merits of digging a foxhole or staying in a small depression that an 88 mm shell hit earlier. Just then another 88 mm shell went screaming by us and landed within yards of where we were. We decided to dig.

The weather was absolutely bitter cold. I now have seen documentaries that say it was 12 above and 12 below zero. Everything was frozen including the water in our canteens. We were all thirsty, including the tank destroyer crew that was parked near us. One of the tank crew took a five gallon can of water that was frozen solid and thawed it out with a blow torch. After melting the ice we drank canteen cups of water that tasted like kerosene. Beggars can't be choosers.

Dusk fell and we continued to dig. Finally, after much effort another G.I. and I were able to carve out a small depression about one foot down. I put my shelter half down with two blankets. We both lowered ourselves down covering up with two blankets. I slept fitfully in a light cold sleep. I snapped awaked from a clicking noise in the dark. Looking around, I saw only shapes of shadows. I asked, "Who the hell is making that noise?" An answer came back to me saying that it was the old man's false teeth. Old man in the army is referring to anyone who is over thirty-five years old.

We stayed on that hill another day and toward the afternoon a guy saw this big German running away from us in the direction of our front left. I didn't see him, but the other G.I. did fire at the German. I said, "He's too far away to hit." Anyway, the German disappeared into the trees. Toward the evening a runner made it through our lines. He said that there was hot chow and some coffee down the hill. We didn't believe him. We felt that we were still cut off. I said, "I'm not taking a chance." The next morning we got word that we were being relieved. We were to head out and go down the hill. That afternoon our relief showed up. We couldn't believe what we saw. A troop of men that looked worn out, dead tired, and with three days growth of beard on their dirty faces. We felt as though we should be their back up! Finally, we pulled out and headed down the hill.

It was dark when we got to our destination. We were walking south now on a narrow road with high hills on the left side. Finally we arrived and stretched out with our backs to the hill and our feet bent just short of the road. I stretched out my legs on the road and felt the cramped feeling of tired muscles relaxing. I was so tired that I did not want to move. A jeep came up the road from the right and stopped just short of my legs. General Van Fleet addressed me in a pleasant tone of voice and said, "Please move your legs." I bent my knees and pulled my feet up without a word. His driver put the jeep in gear and drove off.

After resting and eating we shoved off again going across the country on foot. We struggled up and down snow covered hills. A few green replacements filled our ranks and we took them in hand. One replacement was Lou Sinowitz, a chicken flicker from Brooklyn, New York. He pulled feathers off chicken carcasses. Lou was short, cheerful, and had a roly-poly physique. He was game as we struggled up the steep snow covered hills, but he just could not make it. His legs were not strong enough. A couple of us grabbed him by the clothes on his back and pulled him up with us. Wearily we plodded along in the biting cold toward our destination.

We were on a high hill and were told that there was a large hemp rope that went down the hill over a cliff that ended ten feet above the road that ran along its base. Lowering ourselves down the rope was an exhilarating experience to say the least. What no one told us was that German sniper fire was coming across the valley on the opposite row of hills. Bullets were breaking bits of rock above and below me. That hastened my descent considerably. The G.I. below me cried out in pain as I slid down toward the end of the rope. The rope ended just as they said it would only it was over an outcropping. I had to drop off at the end and pray that I would land correctly. As I hit the ground one of the GI's was attending the fellow who was screaming in pain. He couldn't see where he was wounded. It turned out that the bullet went between his legs and burned his scrotum. I almost ran to my left but got pointed in the right direction to the right. I ran as fast as I could to catch up with the others.

That night we rested, ate, and waited for new orders. I had met a very nice fellow named Stern a few days earlier. We were fast becoming friends. Stern and I bunked down together and wondered what was up for us on the morrow. Our sergeant in charge was named Reams. Early the next morning he told us, "The platoon will head down the plain between the hills toward a town in Luxemburg. Stern will lead, and Sabetay will be the radio man." "What about you?" I asked. "I have other plans," he said. I protested by saying that we would be sitting ducks out there. The Germans were on the hills and in the forest for cover. They were looking right down on us. "Orders are orders!" Reams replied. Later the platoon started out in single file with two scouts and Stern in the lead. We covered about four hundred yards when we stopped. We lay on the ground for three minutes without moving when the word came back that Stern was dead. Back came the reply, "Mission Accomplished. Return to base." It turned out that Stern had been hit by a sniper. He made the fatal mistake of stopping, sticking his head up, and scanning the hill. We were trained to never stick our heads up while scouting out the enemy. If only he had kept moving forward in the unexposed position, he may not have been shot! I really liked Stern so consequently I felt saddened by his loss.

Having returned to our starting point I asked Sergeant Reams why we were sent on this suicide mission. He said that we were chosen to draw fire from the hills while another force of men made an end sweep behind the Germans on the hills to secure the area.

Early the next morning we retraced the route we had started the day before. The only difference was that our flanks were now covered. We trudged the whole day in the bitter cold toward a small town in Luxemburg. Ahead was a wrecked, two and a half ton American truck, with its back wheels blown out from under it. This inanimate object seemed to be silently waiting for us. Next, a wrecked jeep turned up on its side came into our view. We quietly filed past it as though we were paying a silent respect for the job it had done. A Browning Automatic Rifle stuttered three shots into the air. Even the rifles were responding to the horribly cold weather.

Sergeant Reams had drilled me before we left that morning about what he had wanted me to do when we entered the town. I was to run and lob grenades into windows while the rest of the squad would give me covering fire. As we entered the outskirts of the town, Reams changed the plans and said that it wouldn't be necessary. Instead we were to search the houses for enemy troops. Three of us ran up to a house and were beating on its heavy wooden door with the butts of our rifles. We were shouting for the occupants, if there were any, to open up. When no one would open the door I shouted, "I'll fire through the door!" At that very moment someone shouted, "No Bud don't, just wait!" Just then the door opened and a tall smiling Luxembourger stood in front of me. If the cooler heads had not prevailed, I would have been a murderer! After the town had been secured we found out that the Germans had already left. We were welcomed into the Luxembourger's home. He had a warm wood burning stove to defrost our chilled bones. He liked us Yanks because he wanted Nazi Germany out of his country. It felt so good to us to finally have some heat and be relieved from the outside elements for a while. A large salami was passed around to all and it seemed as though it was manna from heaven. Everyone eventually dropped off to a much needed sleep.

The next morning we moved out and headed northward over rolling snow coved hills and forests. Trench foot had hit our men rather rapidly because of the poorly designed American boot. It didn't help that there was no break at all in the weather. We were not allowed to build fires at night for relief from that bitter cold, so the suffering that we had to endure seemed to be enhanced.

Company I of 3rd Battalion was assigned to take a small Belgium town. Because there were only eight men left from the three squads, Sergeant Reams divided us into two squads of four men. We took the town with no resistance at all. A small barn in this area became our temporary home. An important guard post was set up about two hundred yards away. We all took turns manning it. Mail arrived from home and I received a can of anchovies along with a few rolls of Tums. I was so hungry I ate the anchovies like they were a candy bar. Well, let me tell you, I paid the piper for that when my stomach acted like the Revenge of Montezuma.

That evening, Lou Sinowitz and I drew guard duty at the outpost. Dusk fell and the stars twinkled on the cold clear night. We could hear the moaning and utterances of an obvious German somewhere close by. His suffering and moaning filled the freezing cold and otherwise silent night. Lou looked at me and I looked back at him as if to say neither one of us was going to expose ourselves in this situation. In other words, we wondered as to how many other Germans were hiding alongside this poor man. Four hours dragged by and Lou and I wondered why we hadn't gotten some relief from our guard duty. Lou and I stayed at the outpost until dawn started to light up the horizon. Finally we were relieved and I proceeded to ask Sergeant Reams why it took so long. He snidely answered me, "We didn't feel like it." I felt at the time that he was overly tired and he just decided to take a break at our expense. Even though I had experienced some anti-Semitic behavior from other officers, I did not think that Ream's remark was of that nature because he had a Jewish wife.

Later on in the day, we were loaded into trucks and drove through Luxembourg. We disembarked at the outskirts of a city where a few buildings were visible to us. The troops took advantage of this and were resting and generally taking it easy. A convoy of two and a half ton trucks came roaring by. As they approached we strained our eyes to see what they were carrying. It looked like they were loaded with logs. However as they drew closer, I could see that they were the frozen, dead bodies of our GI's. They were stacked to the tops of the side rails of the trucks, which, from a distance looked like cord wood. We watched truck after truck roll by with our dead soldiers. The terrible toll of the war and its consequences struck me very deeply that formidable day.

Orders from headquarters came for us to attack the Germans to the northeast of us. We had the 6th Armored Cavalry on our left, the 26th Armored Cavalry on our right. We the 90th Infantry were in the center. The Luxemburg town by the name of Niederwampack was taken after a 14th Battalion Artillery barrage concentration.

It was at this time that I received a pair of 12-buckle arctic boots from my Dad. He had scoured several stores in the Akron area until he found a pair of size twelve. He ended up finding them at Mason's Shoe Store in Barberton, Ohio. I was able to pull them over my combat boots. What an improvement this would be for me to keep my feet reasonably warm. I thank God that my Dad had been a Canadian Mounty and that he even knew about the arctic boots. A new trick that we learned to help us survive in that brutally cold forest was to change and dry our socks daily. Dry socks were paramount in preventing trench foot. By wringing them out and storing them under our armpits or next to our abdomens, we insured ourselves with a pair of dry socks the next day. Another lifesaving trick that we learned was to get rid of our heavy overcoats. At first I just cut the bottom off of my overcoat but it proved to be too heavy, so I just threw it down on the ground. I learned to layer my clothes in the following fashion; a pair of undershorts and a tee shirt, a pair of long johns, a wool shirt and woolen pants, a wool sweater, a wool hat, plastic helmet liner and a steel helmet on top. This arctic way of dressing was adopted by most of the troops. The biggest disadvantage of belonging to the 90th was the calling of Mother Nature. More than one time I threatened to tie a string around it because the cold had made it so hard to find. The worst was when I had to expose my bare behind to a biting windswept hill when everyone was moving up. Oh well, I wasn't the only one who had to answer the call of nature at an inconvenient time.

It was a very bleak day. I remember we were asked to move up to the side of a road which had a huge flat plain area to the left of the road. As we were walking on the road a woods started to appear on our left. Then suddenly, like something out of a National Geographic appeared. It was a really large buck. He walked along parallel to us. He did not appear to be skittish or afraid. What a beautiful sight for sore eyes he was. Here we were in the middle of one of the last great battles of WWII and one of God's creatures was encouraging us. What a sight this was for the hunters in the group. That old buck walked along our line of march for about a hundred yards and then disappeared back into the forest.

We took another small town. Sergeant Reams, three other soldiers, and I holed up in a basement of an old house. We were famished. Reams found a bin of potatoes and some real honest-to-goodness lard. He said, "We are going to have some French fries!" We proceeded to find a pot, peeled the potatoes, and diced them. My Jewish religion does not permit the eating of lard because it is a pork product, but I think God understood. After all, this was for survival and calories were what we badly needed to fight the brutally cold weather.

The 90th Infantry fought through the Bulge and now focused its attention on the Siegfried Line. The Siegfried Line was similar to the Maginot Line running correspondingly to it. It was already the beginning of February and we had orders to spearhead the taking of the Prum River. Company I of 3rd Battalion shoved off on an attack.

The days were longer then and sunny. We were preparing to meet the enemy and I certainly had butterflies in my stomach. Sergeant Reams went back to headquarters and another sergeant was sent to take his place.

We were moving up over a rolling hill with patches of forest to my right and left when I was summoned by the new sergeant. He said to me, "Fox Company is on our right flank: make contact with them and report back to me." I loped off to the right and kept going for about twenty minutes. I never found anybody. I returned and reported, "No contact." The sergeant was very agitated with me. Ten minutes later, the sergeant called me out and said, "I sent this guy out and he made contact, so why didn't you?" I had no answer but it seemed strange to me that he made contact and returned in all of ten minutes. I wondered in what direction he was told to go. This whole incident seemed very strange to me.

Our company was waiting to push off an attack in broad daylight in front of a big, bald-faced hill. I will never forget this soldier whose name was James. He looked very melancholic and did not easily talk. I asked him what was wrong. He told me that he had not slept well the night before and that he had had a dream that he had been shot and was dying. "Oh, I said, that's only a dream." I rejoined in an effort to cheer him up. Try as I might, I could not shake him out of his depressed state.

All of us were apprehensive about the attack on the bald-faced hill with no cover in broad daylight. At last we started up the hill on attack. As soon as we reached the top of the hill a vicious crossfire pinned us down. The new sergeant and I were together. I had my Model 300 radio on my back. "We can't stay here!" I yelled. "We have to find cover." Below and to our right was a 7-10 foot drop off. "Are you coming?" I hollered. "No, I'm staying here," he responded. "Get under cover!" I urged him. "No I'm staying," he said. "Suit yourself, but I'm leaving." I told him. With that I ran down the hill preceded by a G.I. who was about forty paces in front of me. It looked like geysers of dirt were shooting up at his heels as he ran. A German rifleman was zeroed in on him. As I followed him I felt like a detached observer. The hill came to an abrupt end and he sailed off into the air and dropped out of sight. Running at full tilt, I came to the end of the hill and was hurled into the air. I landed about six feet below on my feet with my radio pack on my back. With the radio on my back, it's a wonder that I did not go head over heels on myself. I took a good bounce but I kept on running spurred on by adrenalin that was riveting though my body. The adrenalin shut off all of the fear and I was able to make quick and accurate decisions.

The two of us crossed a short lawn and dashed into the side door of a house. We found ourselves to be in the kitchen. Glancing around the room, I spotted a doorway that led directly across a hallway and into another room. The hallway that was between the kitchen and the bedroom lead to a door that emptied out onto a cleared area ending with a barn to the right. An overwhelming feeling came over me to check out the hallway; however, a stronger premonition of warning came over me! The strong inner voice proved to be exactly correct, because as soon as I flung myself into the bedroom, a burst of Schmeizer bullet's riddled the door at the end of the hall. Those bullets were meant for me and I knew it! I checked the window that was in the bedroom that overlooked the barn and courtyard and saw no one. Evidently, the German beat it out of there real quickly because he was nowhere to be found. He probably saw us Americans descending onto the house and barn. Shortly after the barrage of bullets, I crossed back into the kitchen. As I looked down the hallway to my left I saw lots of light coming through a large round circle of neat bullet holes.

Across the courtyard was a low-standing, one-story barn. Ultimately a captain, four men, and I ended up in the empty barn. Directly across the door that leads to the courtyard was a small window. This window was really important to us, because we could see the enemy through it. I set up my radio around the corner of that door. The radio was now outside, but I was around the corner on the inside, with the microphone in my hand. Just then a great commotion arose from the window. We spotted a German squad running towards woods that was about three hundred yards from the barn and down a hill. Two of our riflemen shot at the front and the back of the German line but they still disappeared into those woods. Then my Captain called out the coordinates, and I relayed the information to the field artillery, which was up the hill to the left of the barn. A barrage of 155 millimeter shells from our American guns swooshed overhead and dropped into the woods. The guys were jumping up and down in awe recounting the explosions as trees flung through the air. The Germans were catching hell. Everyone had a turn to fire at the Germans.

Ultimately the German high command were aware of our position because shortly after that, a brilliant spot of light from the opposite range of hills came swooshing over our heads. It was so loud that it sounded like we were standing next to a freight train. It missed the end of the barn but a tremendous explosion shook the rafters and our breath was taken away from us for a few seconds. In due course another shell came thundering overhead and striking the hill behind us. "What the hell are they throwing at you?" said this voice over my headset. "Why? I don't know!" I relayed. He said that shrapnel was raining three hundred yards up the hill behind us.

The shrapnel sounded like rain on a tin roof as it came down everywhere, also falling on my 300 radio parked outside of the door. Fortunately it had a strong metal cover and it continued to operate. Our captain sighted the flash of the enemy gun and counted nineteen seconds until the shell came in. This called for stronger artillery from our forces. We used cannons that were big enough to reach out and hit the enemy. We were in the middle of all this crossfire and proved to be a very important part of these two opposing forces. The voice on the radio coming over to me said that he was going to patch me through to the 240 mm Howitzer M1 for counter balance. A 240 mm Howitzer M1 is a cannon that can fire a 360 pound shell 14.3 miles. The lieutenant called for a white phosphorous shell (an incendiary that burns fiercely and can ignite cloth, fuel, ammunition and other combustibles). He gave me the coordinates and I called it in.

Soon we heard a series of shells passing overhead. The captain called out a target, "Fire for effect!" Salvo after salvo passed overhead. (A salvo is a bombardment or deluge of shells coming at you one after another. They are meant to scare you and break you down.) Then there was total silence.

We were to learn later that the Germans were using a Big-Bertha railroad gun. Each gun propelled a shell weighing 2,100 pounds (950 kg) for a distance of almost 9 miles (14 km). They would load it in a mountain and then run it out of a tunnel and onto the railroad tracks and fire it. Then they would reload it back in the mountains again and run it down the tracks again. Needless to say, they stopped firing after we shelled them so overwhelmingly.

A patrol of five men was sent out to go down the valley and across the river. The next morning they showed up carrying a wounded man on a door. They told us they arrived at the Plum River at just after dusk. Across the river was a town with all its lights on and many German soldiers on its streets. Even though a bridge spanned the river, the group of soldiers chose to cross under the bridge in the freezing water. I don't remember how the man was wounded. However, the best part of the story was that they removed a door from a house and carried him back to us that way. Soldiers can be ingenious when their adrenalin is pumping.

The next morning the hill behind us was secured and the rest of the battalion moved up. Our squad returned to the same two story stone and stucco farm house. The only thing that was different about the house was the huge 20-foot hole at the end of the house where the first shell had fallen the day before.

The sun was shining and it was a pleasant day in February. Three of our guys were running around chasing chickens with visions of a great home cooked meal. Three hours later three pots of chicken were boiling on the wood stove. There were jars of cherries, peaches, and pears that had been canned, opened and inviting on the kitchen table. The middle-aged lady of the house came into the kitchen, lifted the lids off of the pots and took one last look at her laying hens. She was wordless and walked out on us. We ate until our hearts and stomachs were content and full.

Sergeant Reams came into the farmhouse and began to question me about the details of the battle. I filled him in, and later he retold the events to a group of soldiers as if he had been in the battle. One of the guys who had actually been in the battle interrupted Reams and said, "Reams, you weren't there so how could you act as if you had been there?" Needless to say that ended that conversation.

I finally was able to find out what happened to James. He was the fellow that I tried to cheer up about his dream. He was shot through the heart on that bald-faced hill. His last words were, "Oh my God, I'm dying!" I also inquired about what happened to the staff sergeant who took Ream's place in the attack. I was told that he was shot in the upper forehead with the bullet exiting the top of his head. He died three days later.

MAXWELL IVEY

We took a break from the fighting for a few days. Replacement troops were sent in but they were very green. We moved on foot through the woods and meadows of Germany in a long line. The sun came out and it grew uncomfortably warm with all the equipment and clothing we had to carry. As we progressed, gas masks, blankets, and other various articles of clothing dotted the ground along our line of march. This ended up stretching for miles.

That night it turned bitterly cold. The green troops were desperate to stay warm. One guy named Maxwell Ivey begged me for a blanket. "Look Ivey," I said, "Why should I give you one of my blankets?

Lt. Ivey with his roaring guns.

I'm the one who carried them!" After much cajoling, I relented and gave him one of my blankets with an admonition to learn to carry and take care of his equipment. I asked him where he came from. "I busted out of OCS,"[4] he said. I don't recall the circumstances of why, but there he was. We became good friends later.

Our next objective was the Siegfried Line.[5] Reams assembled three squads of us and struck off on a night reconnaissance of the line. Our objective was to find a pillbox.[6] Well, we could not find one. The next morning after withdrawing and reviewing our course, we found out to our amazement that we had been standing on

---

[4] *O.C.S.* stands for Officer's Candidate School
[5] The *Siegfried Line* was a line of defensive forts and tank defenses. It was built by Germany during WWI but was revamped and resembled the Maginot Line. It stretched more than 390 miles from the Netherlands to Switzerland. It had more than 18,000 bunkers, tunnels, and tank traps.
[6] A *pillbox* is a concrete fortification like a small house where troops can gather and shoot through small window like openings

one. Reams told us how to secure the area. A guy was to run up to the steel door, place a satchel of TNT there, arm it, and run. All the while, we covered the guy was, aiming at the slits through which the Germans fired to keep them distracted. We *snaked* (crawled on our belly) toward the line through these huge concrete-shaped half gears which had concrete cross-shaped jacks. These were called *saw teeth*. They were placed to stop tanks. All of a sudden all hell broke loose. Tracers filled the air bouncing off the concrete gears and jacks. Just then Reams said that he had stomach cramps and had "to go." I laughed and said, "Damn it, Reams, if you have to go I will cover you." The concrete shapes of the half gears gave us cover. Boy, oh boy, things certainly turned out differently than we had expected.

A few Howitzers were brought up and blasted open the doors. The army engineers did this blasting so that relieved me of doing it. We found out that several of the pillboxes were not even manned by the Germans. It looked as though the Hitler's army was running out of their manned force. Our platoon pressed on with Reams. As we pressed on, we came to a farm house in the middle of the Siegfried Line.

Reams and I got to the farm house where a command post had been set up on the second floor. The captain was peering through his binoculars at the enemy. A G.I. was relieving himself when a barrage of *screaming meemies* hit the farm house. The impact blew the G.I. downstairs with his pants down around his knees. He had a rather sheepish expression on his face directly after the attack. He wasn't hurt and it happened so fast that we all had a good laugh about it. It even broke some of the tension that we were all feeling. "Bud," Reams said, "We've got to go back and find the rest of the platoon." There was a soldier directly behind me but somehow among all the chaos we lost contact. Reams and I left the security of the doorway and got about 30 yards out when something made us stop dead in our tracks. We turned and bolted for the safety of the doorway. As I got to the doorway, Reams bowled me over because he was running so fast.

A barrage of *screaming meemies* hit where we had been. Once again, I felt as though my guardian angel was watching over me. That did not stop us though, because we went out again to the exact same spot. All we found was the front sight from Ream's rifle. I scooped up the front sight and put it into my pocket because my own front sight was askew. I figured out that I could hammer it onto my rifle later. We turned and started doubling back through the Siegfried Line. Just then a German machine gun opened up spewing tracer bullets along our feet. We both dived into a long slit trench, trying to find our buddies. We wanted to take charge of a vacated pillbox. The front end of my rifle barrel hit and got stuck in the mud. Machine gun bullets tattooed up both sides of the slit trench. We were getting it from both sides. Even though it felt like it was 10 above zero, there was still mud from all the action. "Reams" I said, "I'm not going anywhere until I clean my rifle." "Sabetay, you're crazy!" he said.

After cleaning the mud out of my rifle, Reams and I took off running again. A large pair of gate posts appeared. They were made of red bricks about four feet thick, nine feet high, and about eight feet apart. I took refuge behind one of them and Reams the other. A hail of bullets struck the opposite side of both gate posts and bits of bricks went flying. We survived a rather long barrage of that. It finally died down and we took off running again.

Churchill with British and American Generals at the Siegfried Line

We came upon another pillbox and found the rest of our platoon holed up there. One of our guys said that they had fired some German machine guns. We wondered who they were firing at. It could have been Reams and me. The next day we pushed off into the lightly defended line and took several more pillboxes. Our squad holed up in a pillbox that night. A hot meal of chicken was sent up to us. I hungrily wolfed down my chicken but I did notice that a piece of the skin was very salty. That night as we bedded down in the pillbox we saw some German blankets were stacked in a corner. I took my anti bug powder and sprinkled it liberally over my new-found blankets. Then I dropped off into a fitful sleep. I finally woke up in a cold sweat and also felt very nauseated. I felt like throwing up but it was time for me to go on guard duty with Ivey. I stumbled outside feeling just horrible. I was hoping that the cold night air might help me. "Ivey," I said, "I feel terrible. I feel as though I have ptomaine poisoning (food poisoning)." "Go back inside," he said. "I think that I will feel better outside. Just point me in the direction that they are coming from and I will pull the trigger," I said. Ivey said "See that tree out front?" "Which tree?" I asked. Ivey responded, "Bud there is only one tree." I said, "No there isn't. I see four trees." "Boy you really are sick," he answered. I continued to stay out all night which proved to be another blessing because all of the guys in the pillbox had flea bites from those German blankets. I was the exception.

I had a message to take back through the Siegfried Line. I started back walking through the most direct route. I walked through a vegetation patch and happened to look down halfway through and saw stout strings crisscrossing every which way. Weighing only 140 pounds with combat boots, I proceeded through the strings which were only slightly bent. I realized that I was in the middle of a mine field and figured I was nearer to the end, and maybe could make it through. I stepped ever so gingerly through the maze and made it. I picked up my bayonet which I had stashed in a hollowed out space in one of the pillboxes. My bayonet had been in my way, so I took it off my rifle. I was doing lots of close fighting, and it interfered with my sight. In retrospect, I realized it was a foolish thing that I had done. You should keep your bayonet on at all times for defensive fighting.

Every time I passed a dead German soldier in the field, he was in a different position. It seemed that he was rolled over several times. The army engineers moved in and started demolishing the Siegfried Line by blowing up the pillboxes. The results were pillbox roofs lined upside down with torn steel reinforcement bars exposed. There was a feeling now that things were changing for the better for us and the Allied Forces. One day Ivey was being funny by trying to shoot through a K-ration can which was about 75 feet away. He was using a grease gun with a short barrel and a long magazine. The .45 slugs were hitting all around but not hitting the target. "Ivey," I said, "Get rid of that thing and get an M1." With that I drew a quick bead (locate in the sights of a gun) on the can, squeezed one off and blew the can 20 feet high with one well-placed shot. No more explanations were necessary. The sight I used on the M1 belonged to Reams originally. I had hammered it on after hammering mine off with a big stone.

Finally, we got a well-deserved break. Portable showers were set up in the rear echelon and I took a much-needed shower. I luxuriated in the hot water after weeks without bathing. I stayed in the shower longer than most of the troops. We were given clean clothes for the first time in several weeks. In fact we were in continuous battle for 52 days, which would have made it February 15th. Clean and refreshed, we returned to our outfits and waited for our next orders. Mail arrived and I received some socks and handkerchiefs from my Dad. I was so happy that the mail got through. Those socks were a welcome sight.

Our next assignment was clearing the area between the Prum and Kyll rivers. We moved rapidly and seized town after town. One town was shelled with phosphorous shells. The whole town was burning as we raced through the empty streets, meeting no resistance except blistering heat. I ran past a blazing building thinking all the while that this looked and felt like a Hollywood movie. After securing the town we reached the outskirts of it. There, we paused as one of our tank destroyers zeroed its gun on a factory about 1000 yards from us. The tanker sighted on the big brick smokestack and fired one shell. It hit dead center with a puff of smoke and debris. A large hole in the center appeared. It was just great.

Next we moved onto a T-shaped intersection. Our line of men came to a halt arranged along the stem of the T. Racing the cross part of the T from the left, we heard the engine of a motorcycle. It was traveling at a high rate of speed. The line of soldiers waited patiently as a bike carrying two Germans approached the T intersection. As the bike crossed the T, everyone cut loose with a volley of rifle fire. The force of the bullets laid the bike over on its side. The two Germans were dead before they hit the ground. Reams told one of the guys to get the belt off of one of the riders. He returned in a matter of minutes. Later he said that the belt had disintegrated in his hands as a result of all the bullet holes.

Siegfried Line

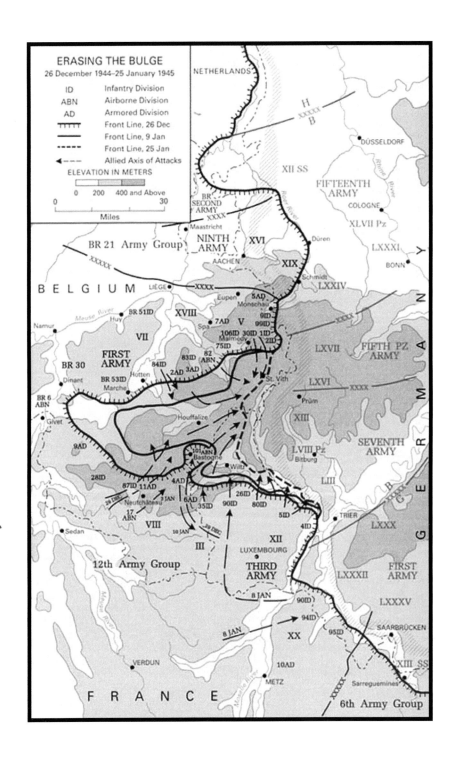

Bud at 88 in 2012

PICTURES OF WAR

Eleventh Panzer Division Surrender

Eleventh Panzer Division Surrender

Eleventh Panzer Division Surrender

Taken in Mainz
Germany after
we cleaned the
hienies out down
to the Rhine
River — we didn't do
much after that
except throw in a
little motar &
Artillery shells as
you can see. A few
fellows picked up
on some target
pradice with rifles

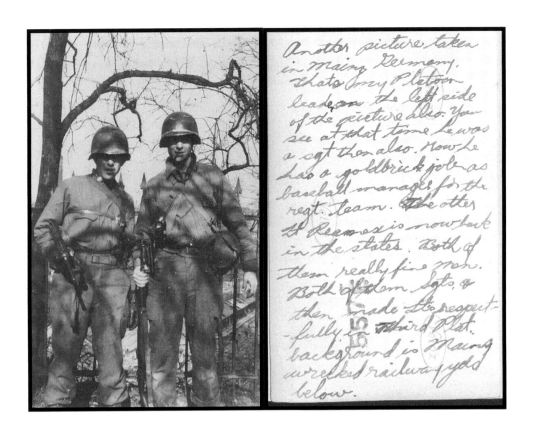

Another picture taken in Mainz Germany. Thats my Platoon leader on the left side of the picture also. You see at that time he was a sgt then also. Now he has a goldbrick job as baseball manager for the regt. team. The other Lt Reames is now back in the states. Both of them really fine men. Both of them Sgts. & then made Lts. respectfully. Third Plat. background is Mainz wrecked railway yds below.

Members of our Squad

In Bischofsheim, Germany just after we crossed the Mainz River. On the right is Fong; on the left is Joe.

Taken in Pressath, Germany on June 6, 1945.

Lt. Scanlan and driver. Note the white flag – Germany's new colors. I installed my radio in the third floor of the house in the background.

Things Beginning to Return to Normal

The Casino du Palais de la Méditerranée on the French Riviera in Nice was taken over by the American Red Cross as a casino and club. The casino still exists today. This picture was taken by a friend on leave after the war around June 1945.

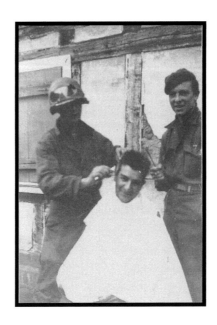

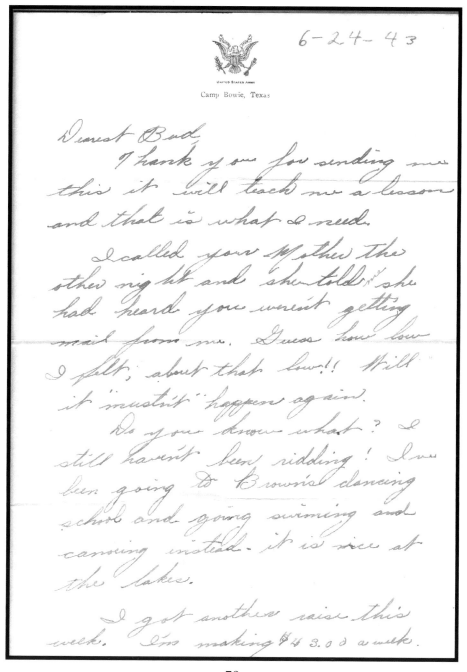

6-24-43

UNITED STATES ARMY

Camp Bowie, Texas

Dearest Bud,

Thank you for sending me
this it will teach me a lesson
and that is what I need.

I called your Mother the
other night and she told she
had heard you weren't getting
mail from me. Guess how low
I felt; about that low!! Will
it "mustn't" happen again.

Do you know what? I
still haven't been ridding! I've
been going to Brown's dancing
school and going swiming and
canoing instead. It is nice at
the lakes.

I got another raise this
week. I'm making $43.00 a week.

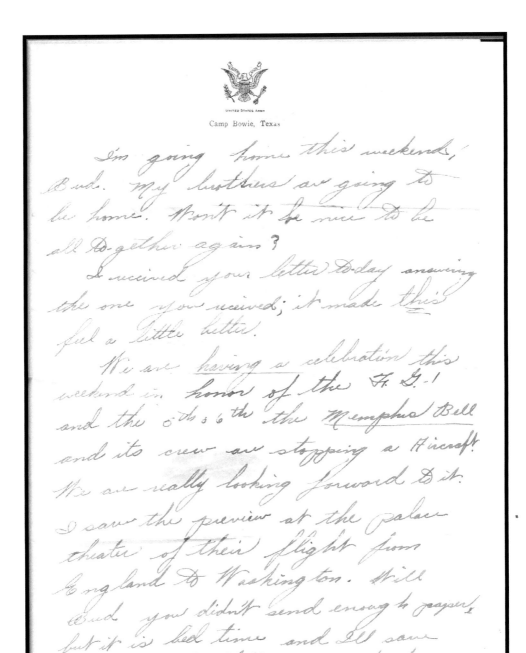

United States Army

Camp Bowie, Texas

I'm going home this weekend, Bud. My brothers are going to be home. Won't it be nice to be all to-gether again?

I received your letter to-day answering the one you received; it made this feel a little better.

We are having a celebration this weekend in honor of the Ft. G. 1 and the 5th & 6th the Memphis Bell and its crew are stopping a Aircraft. We are really looking forward to it. I saw the preview at the palace theater of their flight from England to Washington. Well Bud you didn't send enough paper, but it is bed time and I'll save something to tell you next time.

OVER

80

I almost forgot to tell you that I was transferred to final assembly. I work on the finished planes. All I do is mask the plane, touch up the motor and clean the windows of the cock-pit, getting it ready for the final coat of paint the camoflouge. Write soon.

all my love to a swell guy.

Love,
Jeanie

6-5-44

1.

Dear Dad,

I received your letter on Saturday noon just before I left for Dallas. I saw Mother off Sunday night & then came on back to camp. I had a date Saturday night & Eve & Mike let me use their car. Also I had a date with another girl on Sunday afternoon. She invited me out to a Jewish Picnic. We went swimming

I had a swell time.
Boy does she cut a
mean figure in a
bathing suit.

Incidentaly I am no
longer in 95 Battery, but
have been transferred
to Head Quarters Battery.
The only draw back is
that I have been put
on machine guns & I
am working at it, to
get back on radio.
The fellows are swell
here & I like it very
much. We have a fine
captain who really sticks
up for his men I
understand. There are
seven Jewish fellows
in this Battery now.

3

Something happened
that has aroused my
curiosity of late. I was
informed from a very
reliable source that had
I not transferred into
+2. Battery that I would
have been transferred
clean out of this Battalion.
I put in for a transfer
in 23 Battery about three
weeks after I got there.
Now I am waiting to see
what or where I would
have been transferred if
I remained there.

4

The weather is damnably hot down here. The rats eat you up in the day time & the mosquitoes at night. We won't be here very long though from what I gather. Where or when we move I don't know. But we are due to go overseas anytime now. Overseas furloughs are counted from the last one you received. It has to be six months since. Mine is about 4 months since. I got screwed royal in B Battery; but I sure tried hard to get a furlough. Well thats all for tonight. It's getting dark. Say

5.

Hello to everyone.
With Love
Bud

Dear Mother

I cannot go to South camp tonight & phone you the news, because we are going out on a problem early tomarrow morning. The 1st sgt. called me in & gave me a little hell. He couldn't say much, because I had put him on the spot by signing out. Also I got back at a coporal who I don't like any too well. He got hell because he allowed me to sign out when I was supposed to be on detail. This coporal blew his top & told me that I'd be on extra detail for two weeks. I just laughed at him

& passed it off. But here's the day off. When I got back from radio school this afternoon I discovered I had been transferred to Head-quarters battery. I had been trying for some time to get in H.2 battery; but I couldn't do it. And I had put in for a transfer out of its battery & out of the outfit quite some time ago. In reality though it wasn't through B Batteries efforts that I got transferred, but through a certain influence influential source. There is just one trouble though & that is that I have been put on machine guns. However I think I'll be able to swing it so that I may get on radio again.

3

I'm working on it now.
Mother
~~Father~~ I'll be able to come
into Dallas this coming
weekend or not remains to
be seen, because of the fact
I am a newcomer to H.Q.
battery & I don't know how
the duty roster runs. I might
I might not
draw duty over the weekend.
So stay in Dallas over the
weekend. I might be able to
come in. Also hope this
letter reaches you before
~~I~~ you leave, as I would
feel very bad ~~if it~~ didn't.
Well that's all there is
to write about.

With Love
Bud

Enlisted Men's Service Club
Camp Hood, Texas

Dear All
Be as it may I
have changed hats in
H.Q. astry transferred
so to say to another
light. I now have a
writing table at my
disposal, together with
electric lights, radio &
screened in sides to
keep the other half of
the Texas population
out. I also have a bunk
mate from Kenmore,
Ohio who sides with
me whenever any New
York jerk or New Jersey
language murder makes
a viscious attack upon
dear old Akron, Ohio.

The 1st sgt. & I are
just like that when-
ever any detail comes
along & I eventably find
myself on it. However I
don't let a mere trifle
such as that bother me
I have plenty of time &
believe me I don't break
my strong back for any-
one.

Since we have a
radio in our hut I get
all the latest War News.
My attitude towards the
war is very optimistic
since the Bombing of
Japan again. I have
been doing some
thinking (a rarity I
assure you) lately &

Enlisted Men's Service Club
Camp Hood, Texas

I have drawn this
conclusion. That if we
don't go over soon; that
we'l go over after the
War is over as an army
of occupation. We'll be
more or less a Police
Up Army, might stay
2 or 3 years; So now
I'm hoping that we go
over now; in that way I
figure that we'll be
back sooner. Also after
the War is over I'm
praying that there isn't
any law passed to
make it compulsary
for the young soldiers

to continue on. I have
some mighty ideals
for after the war. I'll
tell you about it after
I see some of my
present
plans pan out now.

Love
Bud

1.

6-19-44

Dear All,

Well it has finally happened at last. We are moving out of Camp Hood very soon. I shan't be able to write you for awhile because we shall be traveling. Also I think that all my mail shall be under censorship & so you'll probably be receiving letters with every other word or so missing. Boy

what a conglameration
you'll probably be
getting.

In your last
letter you mentioned
that Sis might not
be ~~sure~~ coming down
here because of the
heat. Well believe me
it's hot. We run
around without shirts
& hats & still the sweat
pours off our brows ~~to~~
backs.

I have sent two
pictures of our H.Q.
battery & you should
be getting them any
day now. See if
you can find me?

Seriously though it's
fairly definite that
we are overseas bound;
however a lot can happen
between now & then;
you can never be to
sure just what destination
holds in store for you.
I might be able to see
you all before I go
over, I don't know.
We might get shipped
close to home & again
we may not. Strange
as it may seem I do
not find that I am

getting nervous. I feel no tenseness at all. I suppose though that be, ore long that I will get a little hepped up about it. About change of addresses. Well I made out a change of address card for you a long time ago. All I can tell you is to keep sending all forthcoming mail to me until with the old address & it'll be forwarded to me untill you get the change of address cards. I'm closing now with all my love.

From a Guy that
Misses you all
Very Much.
Bud

Jean Powell
423½ Champlain St
Akron, Ohio

Air Mail

AKRON
JUN 30
4 10 PM
1943
OHIO

AIR 6 MAIL
UNITED STATES OF AMERICA

Pvt. Robt. Sabetay 35174386
Batt. B. 773rd F.A. Bn.
Camp Bowie, Texas

Pvt. Robt. Sabetay 35174386
H.2. 7Btry, 773rd F.A. Bn.
Camp Hood, Texas

CAMP HOOD, TEXAS
JUN 6
11 30 AM
1944

free

Mr. David Sabetay
523 Wildwood Ave.
Akron 2, Ohio

INTO THE HEART OF GERMANY

We moved on pressing into the heart of Germany. There was a two-lane road running through the countryside. A high ridge paralleled the road on the left with a clearing of about fifty yards. A dense growth of deciduous trees covered the ridge. As we moved along the road, a patrol of Germans with G.I. prisoners of war were sighted moving rapidly along the ridge some 500 yards from us. Since there was little chance of us catching them we had orders to continue moving up. A lot of us looked back and wondered if we could have saved the prisoners.

It was raining and the road was slick. The motorcade of tanks, jeeps, and trucks came to a slow crawl. A terror-stricken horse with his nostrils flared and eyes wide with fear ran away from the front of the column. He was sliding on the wet pavement. He would fall down in front of the tanks and struggle to get up again. The horse would run a few yards then slip and fall again. Eventually the horse was cleared off of the road and we again moved on.

Town after town fell to our troops. White flags signaled the surrender of the occupants. In many cases the civilians drove out the German troops because they didn't want their towns destroyed. We were moving forward into the heart of Germany when we came to the outskirts of a small city. The houses were dotted here and there along a rolling plain. A row of workers' houses neatly lined up next to each other.

As I moved toward the city there was a fine brick home to my left. Reams ordered me to search it for German soldiers. I broke off from the column of troops and ran into the side door of the house. The German family was just finishing their afternoon dinner as I came bursting in. I ran past them and went upstairs and searched all of the rooms. When I came back down the man of the house offered me something that looked like ginger ale or apple cider. It was March now, the weather was warmer, and I was perspiring and thirsty. I graciously accepted the offer and gulped the drink down. Much to my surprise it was sparkling clear champagne. The man of the house offered me another glass; however, he had to go to an outdoor earth covered wine cellar to obtain it. I followed him out but did not go into the cellar. He came out with a beautiful wicker covered bottle of champagne. Again I found myself in the house telling myself that the war could wait while I enjoyed this fine wine. There were plenty of troops to take care of things. After two more glasses of champagne, the family and I were laughing. We had a good time.

A row of workers' houses had to be searched. There were large, three-foot diameter galvanized wash tubs hanging on the sides of the walls next to the basement steps. The troops broke away from each other and started searching. I started unsteadily down the basement steps hitting my steel helmet on the tubs. I didn't miss a step but I also did not miss hitting those tubs. The German people were laughing now at my folly and I continued on with a grin on my face. By the time we finally finished the search, I had worked off some of that giggly high.

THE MOSELLE RIVER

We were moving fast now. Orders came down to cross the Moselle River located in northwestern Germany. At 2:00 a.m. on March 14th, we assembled on a ridge of the river. We lined up on both sides of the boats. We had a heck of a time with the boats as we slip-slided down the steep slopes of the hill. Finally, we arrived at the river, climbed into the boats, and started paddling. Halfway across the river we landed on a sandbar. Now we were all like sitting ducks because it was almost dawn. We knew at dawn the enemy would have the necessary light to see us. There was nothing for us to do but bail out and start walking across the river in waist high water. The new snow pack waterproof boots that I had gotten were not made for waist high water. At first my feet felt like balloons because of the trapped air in them. And then the water started to leak in and the boots became heavier and heavier. Eventually it felt like I was wearing two lead balloons. Our group made it to shore and started climbing up the steep vineyard hillside. We encountered very little small arms fire. However, our artillery supporting fire was swooshing over our heads and landed about five hundred yards ahead of us on the ridge that was above us. As we progressed up the steep hill in a horizontal line the barrages started coming down the hill about 100 yards at a time. We were two hundred yards up the hill when a salvo landed one hundred yards above us. Reams looked at me and I looked back at him. We knew the next barrage would wipe us out. Reams hollered, "Tell them to cease fire!" I screamed on the walkie-talkie to "cease fire!" with great urgency and much fear in my voice, someone heard me. Thank God the next volley never came.

Our troops worked their way through the vineyards and up the hill. We took a few prisoners and pressed on. My feet were finally starting to dry out. We started climbing up the rolling hills through thick new evergreen trees. You couldn't see through them and we were wet from the snow. These conditions made us very miserable. Eventually we broke out of the evergreens into a mature strand of trees. We were on a high ridge of hills with a valley between and another ridge of hills that ran parallel to us. A lumber mill was down in the valley and our troops started to fire at it. The men who were looking through binoculars at the lumber mill yelled, "Those are our troops!" We immediately ceased fire. You see, our troops were moving into the mill from the opposite range of hills. We just prayed we did not hit any of our own fellows.

At this time we received some green troops into our platoon. One of the fellows I met was a fatalist. He had a philosophy that whatever was going to happen would just happen and there was nothing he could do about it. I had seen enough combat and knew enough about life to make me think that the guy was just nuts. Well, his crazy ideas gave him just what he wanted that very afternoon. He was wounded for the third time and was sent back to the hospital. He was lucky he was not killed. As far as fate goes, I feel that you cannot tempt fate because the next time you do that, it could be your last time to do it. I had a belief system that we had to fight our enemy in order to win and free those who were oppressed.

The 90th infantry went on the offensive. We entered another small town and took control of the city hall. An edict came from headquarters announcing that all cameras were to be turned in. The German populace did as they were told. Hundreds of cameras were turned in and many of our GI's acquired them. We secured that little German town and continued to push on to a train station in Mainz, Germany. There were several German medical officers there who had been captured. They were standing around in front of a train. One man in particular stood out amongst the medics. He was a rather portly man who stood about 6 feet 4 inches. His squinty light blue eyes were surrounded by wispy blonde hair and puffy fat cheeks. Something evil emanated from the smirk on his face. He had a very scary aura about him. It sent a chill down my spine and I felt like leveling him with my rifle.

MAINZ, GERMANY

Our next objective was to take Mainz, Germany. We came across a large hospital which Reams and I entered. We started down a long corridor lined with Gothic style windows on the left wall. The wide corridor was spotless and everything gleamed and shined. There were two ten-gallon bottles of alcohol on gimbals at the end of the corridor. Reams said, "Sabetay, help me take one of these bottles." As we started to lift one of the bottles, a middle-aged nurse in a starched white uniform appeared from the right, hurrying toward us. "Nicht-nicht," she cried out with alarm. We both looked at her and realized that the alcohol must have been very scarce and valuable to the hospital. Carefully we returned the bottle to its stand and left.

We finally came to the outskirts of the town and took a break. We discovered a small house with trees and grass in a rural setting. The house was occupied by a woman and her 12-year-old daughter. The girl spoke some broken English. This girl was at a very innocent stage of her life, so my conversations with her were like those that I would have had with my little sister. Her hair was dark and pretty and so were her eyes. I proceeded to take some pictures of her. She posed for me as I took snapshot after snapshot. What she didn't know was that I did not have any film in my camera. We would eventually move on however, she would probably think that I had some memorable pictures of her. She was happy and I was touched by her happiness. I thought that if I could bring a little gladness into her life by play acting, well, 'so be it.' The Germans were suffering and had been for a long time with Hitler and the whole stinking Nazi machine. If we could bring them a little joy, we felt happy.

Next we entered the outskirts of Mainz and started to search homes. Most of the homes were empty. In one house Ivey and I searched, he found a 120 camera and gave it to me. Next we moved to the center of the town.

Serendipitously, I was walking along a main thoroughfare when I came to an empty major intersection piled high with dirt and debris. As I mounted the debris, I glanced down and right there in the middle of everything was a yellow roll of 120 film. I picked it up and took it with me. The film fit the camera which Ivey had found and I proceeded to take some pictures. A picture was taken of Lt. Reams and me standing on a bridge. He was fidgeting because he was afraid of sniper fire. Another picture was taken of Reams and Ivey overlooking a bombed-out railroad yard. On that very same bridge, we watched in horror as a column of German soldiers were under the white flag of surrender. They then walked toward an American soldier who was going to accept their surrender. We all sensed the evil that could happen next. The lead German dropped the white flag and riddled the American soldier with bullets from a Schmeizer machine gun! We all felt dreadful because we were too far away to warn the American GI. Shortly after that awful horror, we secured the city and our platoon became encamped on the eleventh floor of a building which overlooked the river.

Reams, Ivey, the platoon, and I were moving swiftly through the city when we came to a sparkling burgundy wine plant that was still in production. To our amazement, this plant ran seven stories underground. Needless to say, we captured the factory and took possession of it.

Sergeant Reams and Bud

Sergeant Reams and Ivey

The next morning I took some pictures of our phosphorous shells falling on the other side of the Rhine River. Bowden, a six-foot G.I., looked across the river and saw a bald-headed man peering out of a window of a high rise building. The sun glinted off this man's bald head. Because this bald-headed man was observing us rather closely we considered him to be the enemy. Private Bowden decided that he was going to nail this guy. The sun was very bright that day as I recall, and there was no wind. Bowden laid his M1 rifle on the window ledge, adjusted his rifle sights, took careful aim, and slowly squeezed the trigger. The rifle bucked back on his shoulder as he fired. "Dropped him!" exclaimed Bowden.

Lt. Reams couldn't get that champagne out of his mind. He said to me, "Sabetay, take a contingent of a couple of guys and go get us some of that champagne from that factory we captured." I picked "Doc," a nice guy who just happened to be an alcoholic and another big guy. We were extremely careful where we walked to the factory because of land mines. Upon entering the winery, we were greeted by the supervisor. He was a rather dapper man and of a short stature. He wore a snappy Homburg hat and was dressed impeccably. His English was very good and he conducted us on a tour of the winery. As we passed from floor to floor, amidst the workers, he tried to give us some green champagne. "Nicht, nicht!" said one of the German female workers. I took the warning to heart, turned toward the supervisor, screwed my face into a Humphrey Bogart-like scowl, and snarled in a low voice. "Where is the good stuff?" I said as I shoved my carbine into his stomach. He immediately reverted back to his native tongue of German and said, "Yah, yah." He led us back to the top floor where sealed boxes were coming off the rollers. Believe it or not, the owner had me sign a receipt for the champagne! We helped ourselves to several boxes and started back with our champagne.

By then the Army engineers had moved up from behind the lines; and a lone jeep with one G.I. stopped us and asked where we had gotten the champagne. Doc responded by saying, "You take us back to the front lines and we will tell you." We climbed aboard the jeep and started back. As we slowly drove toward the front lines, the German civilians told us where the land mines were so we would not explode any of them. That night each of us had a bottle of champagne. I proceeded

105

to write a letter home while I got stinking drunk. Needless to say, it was one of the most hilarious letters I had ever written. The end of the letter ended in a scrawl. Later upon passing the winery we saw 2 two and a half ton American trucks lined up and loading case upon case of champagne. I wondered to myself, "Who had signed for that?"

It was during the last day, just before we left, that we disarmed the police. I acquired a German Walther pistol from a policeman. Orders finally came for us to pull out and to cross the Rhine River. We crossed over a bridge and resumed our mad dash into the heartland of Germany. The 359th Regiment was attached to the 4th Armored Division. When we proceeded on, we saw white flags everywhere. These flags had replaced the horrible sight of the Nazi Swastika flags. Riding on tanks and trucks now was a relief from always marching or running. Disembarkation occurred when we came to a small town. We formed a line between and around the tanks and proceeded to take town after town. The 4th Armored was assigned to continue eastward on its own. The 90th, my unit, was also assigned the same mission.

On the move again, we marched toward a small town in a long loose line. It was a wet and drizzly afternoon. There were two soldiers who were wire men crouched over a communication wire that had been severed by an 88 German shell. I had once been in the wire section for the 773rd Field Artillery Battalion. I felt sorry for the men because they were confined to one place repairing the wire. They were under fire from an 88 cannon that had zeroed in on them. The next round found its mark and there they were, two dead wire men sprawled on the ground! As we moved on, we felt very sad for them, but we were also glad that it had not been one of us.

That night we pushed off on attack toward a farm where we knew the enemy was located. It was pitch black and so dark that I could not see the man in front of me. I could only hear him. The one leading us must have had cat eyes because I could not see anything as I stumbled forward. Soon I found myself approaching a huge dark shadow that turned out to be a large stone house. All of a sudden the sky lit up with tracers and 88 shells. A group of us broke for shelter in the barn-like house. As we ran there was a large explosion to my left. A cone-shaped mound of dirt and debris piled up on the floor. A hole of about ten inches on the outside of the wall and three feet on the inside appeared in the two foot cement wall. The building was secured and the ensuing battle was directed from there. The next morning our troops secured a house and barn which overlooked a grape arbor. There was a stretch of land about one hundred yards with more barns beyond that.

Thomas was a GI, thirty-five years old, and hard of hearing. He related a story to me that was funny, and sort of supernatural. It seemed that Thomas was in the heat of a battle when Mother Nature called with 'Montezuma's Revenge.' What better place to go than to an outhouse with the proverbial crescent moon on the door. This particular outhouse was only 75 yards away from the house where they were holed up. Just as he seated himself on the hole, he suddenly developed horrible stomach cramps. As he bent over with a groaning pain, the door of the outhouse was riddled with bullets in a neat round pattern. When he straightened back up he could see the holes that the bullets had made which were exactly where his head had been.

It was morning and I was in a large barn next to the farmhouse. This particular barn overlooked the grape arbor below. I was standing inside a large doorway when a staff sergeant said, "Sabetay, go get the rest of the platoon." "Where are they? "I asked. He said, "They are on the other side of the grape yard in those barns." "But that's 'no man's land'!" I protested. "That area has not been cleared yet." "I know." he answered. "But you have to go and bring them back." I stalled as long as I could. I could not help but think that I was a sitting duck for a slaughter. Finally after much trepidation, I took off in a dead run racing through narrow paths. I was weaving through the grape arbors and finally broke into a clearing where the barns were. This whole obstacle course was about 40 yards or so of weaving and running. It seemed to me that I was chosen quite a bit as a scapegoat for dangerous maneuvers. "Sabetay," the squad hollered, "Where did you come from?" "Through the grape yard," I answered. "But that's 'no man's land'," they shouted. "No it isn't." I said, "The Germans have left!" I proceeded to lead them back without an incident.

A large American soldier, standing about six feet tall, 35 years old, and weighing about 200 pounds, was wounded in the chest. He desperately wanted some water. We were told not to give him any because we did not know if the wound had penetrated the pleural or the peritoneal cavities. He was really upset about the water. What we couldn't figure out was how he was able to go through battle with that serious of a wound.

We continued to push eastward and took town after town. Reams, two other guys, and I occupied an upstairs apartment in a small town. I had a 300 radio and Reams told me to listen for orders. Reams and the two others sacked down. I had to stay awake all night and keep my eyes and ears open. I found this hard to do because I was extremely tired from all the battles. We had been on the go without a break for at least two days.

About two o'clock in the morning I was startled wide awake by a scared and trembling voice coming over the air waves. "The Germans are coming and they are coming up the stairs, and they are outside of the door!" Then there was dead silence. What was puzzling to me was that the soldier did not identify where he was. I thought that he assuredly had a rifle. Why didn't he fight back? This could have been a psychological ruse to scare us. We shrugged our shoulders, because there was nothing we could have done anyway. We felt sorry for him if it was true, but if it wasn't then the ruse had failed.

The next morning we were on attack. American tanks were going up a narrow mountain road. The mountain wasn't very big but it was very treacherous. The mountain was on the right and the road was on the left. Our American tanks were roaring up the mountainous dirt and rock road. It was a steep vertical rock of a mountain. Germans were sniping at us from the high ground on the right. We took cover on the left side of the tanks where we hung on and were half dragged and pulled along. We persisted and survived.

Ivey pulled out a captured German map and said, "If I take a group of men around to the other side of the mountain we can surprise them." With that he took off with a small group of G.I.s and disappeared around the other side of the mountain.   Sometime later he returned, triumphantly saying, "Mission Accomplished!"

The following day we were on a plain and moving toward a large, Greek-style house with Doric columns that were two stories high.   As Ivey and I approached the house, he asked if I would carry his pair of 750 Zeiss binoculars for him. I retorted, "If I carry them, you can use them, but they are mine, agreed?" He reluctantly agreed and that is how I acquired a pair of beautiful German field glasses.

Later we secured the big house and some German prisoners. I had the opportunity to talk to one of the German prisoners of war. He was gravely wounded and was awaiting transport to a hospital. The man spoke English and this was his story he related to me. He had been an artist and then drafted into the German army. He was also highly educated and ended up in the *Wehrmacht*. The Wehrmacht, otherwise known as the regular German Army, were the unified armed forces of Nazi Germany from 1935 to 1945. It consisted of the Heer (army), the Kriegsmarine (navy) and the Luftwaffe (air force). Such are the fortunes of war. I was very curious about the enemy and spoke softly to him in English. I felt sorry for him because he was in so much pain. It seemed that the Wehrmacht wasn't much better or different than us.

We were on the move again through the fields and farms of Germany. Our squad came to a group of farm buildings, an old house and a small barn. There was a well with a pump near the barn. Being very thirsty, we filled our canteens and then began drinking the water. I almost gagged as the taste hit my tongue. Castor oil tasted better than that water. However, since we were short on water we took it and vowed to change water at the first opportunity.

A group of us advanced across the grass-covered rolling fields. It was probably around April and at least the ground was not muddy. It wasn't that cold anymore like it had been. We were all satisfied with the weather. We were going in the direction of a road that was raised off the ground about two feet. As we started walking single file along the road we encountered machine gun fire at our foot level. This dirt was popping up at the right sides of our feet and the dirt geysers were only about six inches apart. Needless to say we were all scared of losing our lives. Without a moment's hesitation four of us dove over the two lane highway to the other side. Now we were protected by the road because we were beneath it and behind us was a hill with a railroad bridge running on top of it. One G.I. stranded himself by laying belly down on the road. Those machine gun bullets had scared him to death. He just would not move even though I urged and cajoled him. I even reached up and touched his arm and coaxed him to take cover with us. "No," he said, "I'm not moving." I protested, "You're a sitting duck, roll over down here with us." "I'm not moving," He said again.

Ivey grabbed a Browning Automatic Rifle (BAR) and shouted that he was going up on top of the railroad bridge to give us covering fire. I'll tell you, that Maxwell Ivey could think fast in a crisis and was also a fearless fighter along with being a great guy. He took off running through the bridge and got to the other side of it. He laid down on the railroad tracks, leveled his weapon and opened up. The deep rumble of the BAR firing overhead really gave us comfort. Eventually, Ivey came back. We all got up and convinced the G.I. on the road that it was OK. We moved on.

We eventually rejoined our battalion and continued to move forward into Germany. Our squad approached an American tank on the rise of a little hill. It was overlooking a two lane road running directly away from us toward enemy territory. The road was lined by evenly spaced, oval-shaped mature trees. There was a column of some 20 German soldiers walking toward us. They were about 400 yards away and did not see us. The tanker on top of the turret said, "Watch this!" He pulled the bolt back, depressed the trigger of the 50 caliber machine gun and fired a long burst of bullets at the column. German soldiers peeled off right and left to the side of the road. Retribution was sweet.

We had a brief lull in the battle. This break was welcome because the whole company had diarrhea. The medics set up in a small one-story building with a steep pitched roof. There was a stairway into the building with three steps in the front and the same in the back. Hundreds of troops were lined up on the plain in front, two columns deep extending back at least a half of a mile. There was another half mile of troops departing the back door. We were all hoping for relief from this horrible curse. My turn finally came. Two of us mounted the stairs and were immediately approached by two doctors asking us what the trouble was. I explained my dilemma to him and for standard course of treatment he ordered me some paregoric. I said to him, "It doesn't seem to be working. Is there anything else I can take?" He hesitated for a moment and then said, "Yes, you can take Epsom salts orally. I answered, "How does it work?" He responded, "It will clean you out." "I'll take it," I said. After swallowing the Epsom salts I left the building. True to the doctor's word, it cleaned me out and I was cured. Unfortunately, those who took the paregoric were still suffering.

We were on the move again. This time we were moving down a long sloping two lane road. The roads in Germany were bad but they saved my life many times. There were a few tanks in front of us with the troops strung out for a half mile. Now we came upon a shallow dip in the road and then it gently rose slightly again with a bridge straddling it. Just beyond the bridge I could see an American tank stranded on the top of the rise of the road. Heavy caliber shells were whistling up the road toward us. We were strung out in ditches on both sides of the road. There was a group of men on the other side of the road in a clearing. They were gathered in a circle around a nice bonfire, obviously warming up as they waited for the road to clear. A heavy mortar shell dropped from the enemy into the center of the fire and kicked up a few pieces of wood; however, it was a dud and did not go off. With a live mortar shell in the center of the fire the troops scattered and gave the fire a wide berth. Blocking the forward advance was that American tank. It had been hit and abandoned. I wondered why someone didn't mount the tank and man the fifty caliber machine gun on the top which was still intact. I contemplated running up the road and mounting the tank to give cover fire, however, I was at least a quarter of a mile away. With heavy caliber fire whistling up the road I decided that prudence was the better part of valor. Finally a G.I. did mount the tank and manned the machine gun and started firing at the Germans.

Eventually we moved up the road and passed the tank. Off to our left we saw three 88 millimeter field artillery in a semi-circle aimed toward us. They were about 50 yards from us. The G.I. who had finally manned the 50 caliber gun on the tank did an incredible job.

After securing the enemies 88 caliber guns we moved out to the countryside where there was a long, low one story warehouse. My platoon was spread around the perimeter of the inside of the building. We took a much needed break and were all shoving down K-rations. A mortar shell dropped through the center of the roof and exploded. The men who were directly to my right and to my left were both critically injured. They fell over and didn't say a word. I continued eating because the medic was attending to them. At this point of the war, I felt numb to what I just witnessed. Lieutenant Reams (just promoted from Sergeant) seized the moment and said, "Stay calm like Sabetay is doing." The men calmed down and the medic administered first aid.

"Sabetay," Reams called, "Head down the hill to the base where there is a medical station and bring help." "Yes sir," I responded. By the time I reached the bottom of the hill (about a mile from where I started), I was panting hard and out of breath that I could hardly speak. Between pants for breath I gasped out that there were men hit in the warehouse near the top of the hill. The medics told me to catch my breath and they would send up stretchers to bring them out.

A MIRACLE

After recovering my breath, I trotted back up the hill toward the warehouse. I had covered about 400 yards when I spotted Silk coming down the hill toward me. He was about eight yards in front of me when I heard some woman's voice say, "Buddy, think of something! Do it now! Silk is in great danger!" I had to think of something quick so I said to myself, "I can tackle him." Prompted by instinct, I tackled him and we both rolled down the hill together. As we were rolling, a mortar round fell exactly where Silk had been. "Silk," I said, "What are you doing here?" "Reams sent me down to find out what was taking you so long," he answered. "Just one question," Silk said, "How did you know to tackle me when the mortar round was coming?" "I don't know," I answered him. "I heard something and I just reacted." At that time, I was too embarrassed to tell him that I had heard an audible voice. Having heard my childhood nickname in a loud audible voice had me in total wonderment.

Both of us returned to the warehouse together and reported in. The stretcher bearers finally arrived and carried the two wounded men to the hospital.

We were on the move again. The next morning our company captured an egg warehouse. The field kitchen was brought up and we were treated to eggs any way that we wanted them except for boiled. How refreshing that was compared to K-rations. The warehouse was a one story building on the outskirts of a city. The company took a break because we had been moving fast. We were due for a rest.

The 90th Division was now in the heartland of Germany. We were moving east and cutting Germany in half. We now captured a one story factory warehouse. It had factory-style steel sash windows that were stacked all the way to the ceiling. There were also rows of tank engines lined up neatly down the center length of the building. Aisle upon aisle of engines was all you could see. There was something wrong with all of them. They all had pin holes on the top of the heads because the Germans had poured acid on the manifolds and heads. The Germans were not using them but they did not want us to use them either.

Our squad came across little black square rubber blocks. These blocks were 4x4x4 inches. I have forgotten how they were used in the tanks but interestingly enough they had a bounce about four times that of a rubber ball. We sure had some fun bouncing them around.

Late one evening we came across an inn located in the woods. It was about 150 feet long by 40 feet wide. We climbed the stairs to the second floor. Upon reaching the landing, we saw the whole second floor was filled with wooden tables and captain's chairs. We quickly formed a line of soldiers, stretching from one end of the room to the other. Tables and chairs were passed from one end of the room to the other, where they were tossed out the large window at the end of the hall. After that, we had plenty of room for everyone to stretch out and get a good night's sleep. Everyone was tired after being on the move day after day with little sleep. I never knew what day or month it was. There was no time for us to keep track of days and months. I do remember the weather was better and there was no snow on the ground.

The next morning I was curious as to what it looked like at the end of the building on the outside. It looked just as I had imagined it. Tables and chairs were stacked helter skelter - ending in a pyramid just below the second story window. They looked intact and like most of them could be salvaged. I didn't imagine though that we endeared ourselves to the innkeeper.

The platoon was moving through a hardwood forest when we came across a German Luger pistol laying on its right side. We came to a halt and tried to determine if it was a booby trap. Silk took a long slim branch from a tree and probed cautiously all around the pistol checking the ground for a trap. After what seemed to me to be many tense minutes, Silk secured the pistol and we moved on.

A short time later we took charge of a small farm and our squad bunked down on the second floor of the house. There were broken-down German trucks about fifty yards from the end of the house. Ivey secured the trucks' batteries, small light bulbs and sockets. He arranged them in a string of bulbs which looked very much like lighted Christmas lights. It was an overcast day and the light bulbs came in handy for writing letters. I thought it was neat of Ivey to figure out something that useful. In the house with us was a German man who was about 30 years old with straight dark hair and of medium height and build. He said that he could make a shoulder holster for my German Luger which I had acquired from Silk. When I got the finished holster it fit my shoulder and body well but it took a major effort to remove the gun from the holster. It was made too small for the pistol. There was something about the man that Ivey didn't like. He told me not to pay him because the holster was too small.

Shortly after our stay in the house, we were pulled away from there and given additional training. This consisted of arming our rifles with blanks and shooting grenades from the end of our rifle. The butt of the rifle was planted on the ground and the barrel was pointed almost perpendicular toward the target. A fitting of the end of the rifle barrel held a grenade. The khaki colored tube was about seven or eight inches long and one and a half inches in diameter. We were situated on a ridge with sparsely spaced deciduous and evergreen trees which overlooked a hut, some two hundred yards below us. By adjusting the barrel of the rifle forward or backward and from side to side, I was able to bracket the hut which was about 12' X 12' and only ten feet high. Try as I might, I could not drop one on the center of the roof. I thought I had become pretty proficient, however, as it turned out, I never did have an occasion to use a rifle grenade.

We were off again. This time we were strung out and climbing snow covered mountains. We were snaking up a narrow trail when we came to a sparsely covered ledge near the edge of the tree line. This is where we took a break. We broke out our canteen cups, scooped up some snow and set them on little tins with pellets that acted like sterno cans. The high altitude prevented the sterno from getting hot enough to make coffee because of the lack of oxygen. The water only got lukewarm in that thin air. Try as we might, the powdered coffee just wouldn't dissolve in that lukewarm water. To make matters worse, I stuck my hand into my pockets and they got stuck into this gluey stuff which was the powdered coffee. It had burst its vacuum in that high altitude. Oh, how we all wished for a good hot cup of coffee, but it just didn't work out.

We finally reached our objective - a ski resort. The building was secured with no resistance at all. The Germans had left. The main ski building was large, gray, and wooden, with a huge pitched roof. The windows were large double windows. That was the first time that I had seen insulated glass in a building.

I was headquartered in this building with a first lieutenant and other NCOs (non-commissioned officers), because I was a radio operator. A pretty German girl was somehow left behind. She was a petite, good looking, slender woman with dark wavy hair and dark eyes. It was apparent to me that she was left there as a spy to seduce us men and probably relay information to the Germans.

All of us took it easy for a day and then proceeded to get our orders to move on. A long line of G.I.'s, including myself, snaked down the mountain past a high ski jump. A shot echoed down the mountain and a G.I. dropped dead in the snow. The column stopped. A squad of soldiers turned back and retraced their steps back up the hill. They were going to the small village we had just left. About a half hour later they returned and we moved down the mountain again. Word passed back that a ten-year-old was found in a church steeple with a rifle. Suffice it to say tempers ran high and the ten-year-old was no longer around to brag about his exploits. Combat justice has no respect for age.

A few days later I was with a group of GI's attacking a small town. The street stretched in front of me with a clearing: and a group of buildings. A soldier on my right yelled, "There is a German aiming his rifle right at you!!" "SHOOT HIM!" I yelled as I dodged to make myself as small of a target as I could. He fired and the German was no longer a threat. In combat someone may see something you do not see and vice versa. Although I appreciated the warning, I wondered why he didn't take immediate initiative and fire sooner.

We worked our way through the town when Reams and I came across a big German soldier. He was about 6 feet 2 inches lying face down on the ground with his arms and legs churning in slow motion as if he were running. The unusual thing was that he had a *potato masher*, (a German hand grenade) in his right hand. It was approximately 14" X 4" with a wooden handle and a metal canister. This particular grenade had a black stripe on it. Different grenades had different colors on them denoting the number of seconds before they were to detonate. Evidently, this soldier had not armed the grenade probably because he was shot down before he could throw it. The German soldier's head was ashen gray in color and his body was going through a running motion, as if it were on automatic pilot. Reams said, "Where should I shoot him to put him out of his misery? His grenade is liable to go off." "Shoot him through the temple!" I told Reams. He pointed a .45 caliber Grease Gun and shot several rounds into his left temple. The German soldier's body kept moving while his arms and legs were still running in slow motion. "Sabetay," Reams said, "did you see the bullets go in?' "Yes Reams," I said, "I saw them but I don't know why he isn't dead! "Leave him and let him die in peace." I know that I felt really sad for this German soldier and pretty sure Reams did too or he would not have asked me where to shoot him. After all, Reams was a lieutenant now and did not need my OK to shoot the enemy. That whole incident seemed to be the nature of war. We all had to do things that were not so black and white, especially in those of which we had no control.

We moved on and were snaking our way up another mountain in a single file. It still bothered me greatly as to when the German soldier would die. I passed word down the line and asked if the German had died yet. The answer came back, "no." A little while later I passed word down again. This time the answer was, "Yes, he died." It bothered me that he did not die immediately when Reams first shot hit him. In retrospect, he probably was already brain dead when Reams shot him.

As we assembled and moved up the mountain, Ivey pulled me aside and said, "Bud, if something happens to the company, we will take it over." I answered, "OK," but I was thinking at the time that this was a strange statement for Ivey to make. The company started to climb single file up a narrow path flanked by a narrow bank of grass and mature pine trees. We slowly continued upward for about one and a half hours. We had reached the peak of the mountain. Two scouts were ahead leading the way. The First Lieutenant and my radio-carrying self were about two yards behind. Machine gun fire sliced through the thin air, pinning down the two scouts ahead and the lieutenant just ahead of me. The lieutenant lay just below a rise which naturally flanked him on both sides of the path. Tracer bullets were painting orange streaks inches above his derriere with crossfire from two directions. I lay to the left of the First Lieutenant, so close that I could reach out and touch him. My heart was pounding so hard that I felt like it was hitting my ribcage. I was just waiting to spring into action, but there was no command issued by the lieutenant. The lieutenant lay there throwing up and writhing in pain. "Lieutenant, we have to move out!" I said. "You are not in any condition to lead us," I said. "Yes I am! I'll be alright, "he responded. "No you're not! 'I retorted with concern in my voice. "I'm sending back for Ivey!" A few minutes later Ivey appeared running in a low crouched position. He surveyed the scene and asked me to fill him in on a few details.

Ivey took command, moved us forward and we attacked a lodge full of Germans. We secured the lodge with many prisoners who were wearing Red Cross Armbands. It seemed strange there were so many Red Cross aid men in there. Finally, some other officers from our rear arrived and took over this scene. There were many regular Wehrmcht and German Pioneer troops captured. In this group were about eight Wehrmacht troops, some were middle aged and some younger. They had to be taken down the mountain to a holding compound. A private, who had been booted out of the Air Corps on a Section Eight and sent to the infantry, was assigned to take the prisoners down the mountain. The prisoners were lined up single file with that private behind them. They were headed down the mountain when we heard a series of shots ring out echoing through the mountains. It was an eerie sound to say the least. Ten minutes later, the private returned alone. When asked what happened, he responded, "One of them tried to get away, so I shot them all!"

After that episode, none of us had anything to do with him. Whenever this guy was among us, no one spoke to him or answered him. A strange silence walled him off from us from that day on. I believe, as did my buddies, that he had committed murder. We saw quite a bit of this going on from both sides. Lots of our G.I.s were murdered by the Germans. It was sickening to think that we were living amongst a murderer. War was one thing, but murder is another.

Thinking back to us going up the mountain, I had wondered what prompted Ivey to anticipate taking over the company. He must have been aware of the situation before it occurred. Because of that occurrence, Ivey received a battlefield commission. Ivey had the background in the OCS (Officer Candidate School) plus the intelligence and the grit to become a first class officer. He might have been booted out of OCS but he did attain battlefield status. And that was where it counted.

THE DEATH OF PRESIDENT ROOSEVELT

The company was pulled out of action on April 15, 1945, and sent into a small German town that was previously captured. We were herded into a medium size Gothic church where we learned that President Roosevelt had died. Prayers were said on his behalf. We all were in a bit of a shock and a silent sadness overcame the troops. As I look back now, I wonder if President Roosevelt knew how close we were to Victory in Europe Day (VE Day) before he died. It was less than thirty days away. President Harry Truman was our new Commander and Chief, but we did not know a whole lot about him. He certainly proved himself to be one of the best presidents that our country ever has had. The chaplain led us in prayer for him also. He prayed and we agreed that God would give him the strength and the fortitude to see us through to victory. History has proven what a good, wise, and fair-minded, man that he really was. I know we all ended up admiring him.

President Truman

The weather was wet and miserable as we left the church. We walked a short distance and came upon a movie theater. A 20th century newsreel brought us up to date as to our success worldwide and a little propaganda was thrown in as to why we were fighting. I had been fighting from Christmas Day until now. I was not aware of the date, the day of the week, or even what month it was. There was no time for thinking; only time for fighting, trying to stay alive, and to keep your buddies alive.

The company returned to the offensive line again. Our battalion was given orders to take a small village in the mountains. Reams lead the way with two scouts out in front, and then it was my turn to take the lead. We labored up a stony ridge with mature pine trees growing thick on either side of our path. It was very early, about 4:00 a.m. We tried to make as little noise as possible because we were on a sneak attack. Loose rocks slipped from under our boots and an occasional clanking noise emanated from a rifle slapping against our bodies. The weather was cool but we didn't notice it much because we were sweating so profusely going up that ridge of loose rocks.

A MOUNTAIN VILLAGE

Dawn came peeping over the mountain as we approached the village. Our platoon finally broke into the outskirts of the village. The village was nothing more than two-story stone and brick houses spaced closely to each other. There was no resistance to us as we passed several houses. At the intersection of two roads was a two-story house. Reams commanded me to throw a grenade into the basement window. I had an incendiary phosphorous grenade hanging on my fatigue jacket's lapel. The grenade slipped easily from the lapel hole into my right hand. I was ready to toss it into the basement, but there was a problem. I proceeded to pull the ring out of the grenade with my left hand. But, no matter how hard I pulled on it, I just couldn't get it out of the main part of the grenade. "Reams," I muttered, "I can't get the damn pin out!" "Never mind," he responded, "Let's get out of here."

In the meantime, we came upon a white stucco house which was about forty yards from the two story house with the significant basement window. We entered a large living room to our right with a stone floor and a huge, imposing, stone fireplace. To the left was a large dining room with a long wooden table and chairs that could accommodate 10-12 people. This table was set with dishes and there was steaming hot food in them. However, the house was empty and no one was in sight. At that point I tried to make contact with the command center with my walkie-talkie, to no avail. I thought if I could get into the fireplace I could get reception on my radio. That worked out well and I made radio contact with the company and reported in.

The village was finally secured. We learned later that the women and children of the stucco house were in that basement of the first house where I unsuccessfully tried to throw the grenade.

That grenade I tried to throw into the basement of the first house was barrel shaped, about seven inches long, and about two inches in diameter. This was the same grenade that swung up from my lapel. Whenever I would run it would strike my front tooth and actually chipped one of my front teeth. This grenade had a very loose pin. I was always afraid the pin might get caught on something when I was crawling. It could have come out, armed the grenade, and caused it to go off. I took my bayonet and spread the end of the pin that was shaped like a cotter pin. Before shoving off on this attack, I bent it straight again. However, it was bent enough that I couldn't get it out no matter how hard I tried, as I said. When a phosphorous grenade explodes, it burns anything it touches. It will continue to burn when it strikes the flesh and it can burn a hole right through you. I shudder to think what it might have done to those women and children who were in that basement. At that point, I was so glad that the pin did not work.

A stone castle on the crown of the mountain at the end of the village was secured. The owner was about 60 year's old, lean, weather-beaten, and about 5 feet 10 inches. He was run down the mountain by a fellow soldier by the name of Sorenson. Sorenson was a big 6 foot 4 inch Swede with red hair, broad shoulders, and a huge frame. He ran the German down the mountain with his chest pushing himself into the enemy's back. When I asked him why he did it that way, he answered, "Because I felt like it!" I think that Sorenson just wanted to blow off some steam.

Two beautifully engraved shotguns were released when we reached the rear echelon. They were packed and sent home as war trophies by two G.I.s. We pulled out of there, while at the same time; Reams put me in charge of the platoon. I took us out the same way we had come, in spite of the fact that an easier path was reported to me. There was much grumbling and complaining but Reams backed me up to the hilt. A premonition came over me again, and I felt I was instinctively protecting our troops. Reams wanted to make me staff sergeant. I said to Reams "I think not! "When I became an infantry man I was a private, not a private first class, just a private! Not even a good conduct metal! I am a P.F.C. now, have a good conduct medal and a combat infantry man's badge. Since I have been in this outfit they have gone through eight sergeants. I'd rather not be a sergeant at this time." Being a radio operator had its advantages. I was with an officer most of the time. I didn't draw guard duty, didn't have to lead the platoon as a point man, and didn't have to go on patrol. If the officer found a house to stay in, I also stayed.

MORE COMBAT

We had the village and went down the mountain where trucks were waiting for us. The company took a break behind the lines for a few days. We were given orders to shove off on attack. This time we attacked through a forest of huge trees with open spaces between the trunks. Troops were spread out in front, to the side, and the back of me. We were all running hard with rifles toward the enemy. A soldier materialized running toward me in the opposite direction. Thrusting my arms straight out his shoulders bumped hard into the palms of my hands which jolted him to an abrupt halt. "Where are you going?" I demanded. "Back!" he said. "No you're not!" I shouted, "You are going forward with me!" I proceeded to slap him hard with the palm of my right hand. As my arm swung past his face, I backhanded his face on the down stroke. Swinging him around by the shoulders, I kneed him in the butt and he stumbled forward. "That way is the front lines!" I shouted, "I'm right behind you." He trotted off toward the front lines more afraid of me than the Germans. I lost sight of him as he was running through the woods.

Shots rang out and a G.I. fell to my left. His legs were knocked under him by a bullet he took to the hip. Diving belly down behind a huge tree with big roots, I picked myself up and headed for another tree which was 30 yards in front of me. However, the second tree I picked as an alternate was 15 yards closer. A rifle bullet made a popping noise as it passed over my head. Again I ran full tilt toward the enemy and suddenly saw a German in a blue airman's uniform. I couldn't fire at him because our G.I.s were running in front and to the side of me. I was afraid that I would hit one of our own men. The German was 300 yards ahead and disappeared amongst the trees.

A patrol was sent out to see where the 20 mm shells were coming from. What they found was a tank instead of an armored car. Sneaking up behind the tank they took careful aim and fired a bazooka. The bazooka was caught in the grill work of the back of the tank. The turret swung around and the patrol of eight men was seen soon running back to us. We were ordered to make a strategic withdrawal, what is commonly called an *advance to the rear*.

I was the last man to leave the scene after I relayed the message that trucks were waiting for us. There were 88 mm shells screaming in and hitting the trees about twelve feet up the trunks. The tops of the trees would drop across my path as I scrambled desperately to catch up. I guessed that the tank found the range that it needed. As I jumped tree trunks, dodged, and twisted, I found myself among the first troops to reach the waiting trucks. We were pulled back behind the lines and took a break in a row of new brick houses on the outskirts of a city.

THE ELEVENTH PANZER DIVISION SURRENDER

Ivey and I bunked down in a nice brick bungalow. It was totally deserted as were all the other row houses. I was absolutely famished. Ivey looked in the kitchen cupboard and found a box of split peas. "Bud, I'm going to make you some split pea soup," he said. True to his word, Ivey whipped up some split pea soup. I would say that soup was the most delicious soup I had ever eaten. We spent one night there. The next morning Ivey and I took some pictures of each other and looked forward to spending the next two days just relaxing. However, this was to be short-lived. Orders came down calling us up again to the front lines. We protested, "We just got here!" They said that there was something about the elite Eleventh Panzer Division. "Why can't somebody else accept surrender?" We wanted to know. "Because the 11th Panzer Division won't surrender to any other division, only the 90th Texas Oklahoma Division," they replied.

Surrender of the 11th Panzers

We reluctantly returned to the front lines to accept the surrender. We did not know, nor were we conscious of the fact that we were involved in making world history. I found myself standing along a narrow two-lane road opposite a row of houses on a rolling countryside. American troops, at least 100 of us, were arrayed in single file along both sides of the road. A long line of German soldiers, some in trucks, others in horse-drawn wagons were making their way right down the middle of the road. It was a sight for sore eyes. I had really never seen a two-horse-drawn wagon before. It was loaded with Germans. There were only a few cars and some armored cars. This went on for hours. I noticed that the soldiers were clean shaven and their uniforms were immaculate. They had real pride and displayed a lot of class as to how they would look to us. In contrast, our troops were not clean shaven and our uniforms were anything but clean. Another thing that was a glaring sight to me was that the elite 11th Panzers equipment was worn, patched, and almost nonexistent. We were clearly the victors. I thanked my lucky stars and felt relieved that I wouldn't have to fight them anymore. Intuitively, I felt that the war would be over very shortly.

That day, as I remember it, was a dreary, overcast, cold day. My fingers were poking out of the ends of my leather, fur-lined gloves. They were a gift to me from my sisters. A German officer in a small car passed by me slowly. He noticed me squeezing water out from my gloves. He leaned out the window and handed me a new pair of gray ski mittens with a trigger finger. I thanked him in the German language. I believe he had been a good officer and that his pity was his way of saying, 'you beat us fairly and squarely.' Needless to say, I was very grateful for the warm mittens.

It was later that day that we learned why they surrendered to us. Every engagement the 11th Elite Panzers had with the 90th Texas Oklahoma Division was formidable because they had to go back and reorganize each time. We didn't know that we were that tough. Pictures were taken of the surrender by one of our soldiers. Later I acquired the negatives and had the pictures developed. They are in my possession to this day. Another thing that was done that day was the burning of hundreds of Mauser[7] rifles that were stacked in piles along the roadside.

Eventually over 9000 German troops surrendered on May 4, 1945. The 90th Infantry was ordered to spearhead a drive to capture Prague, Czechoslovakia. We had to clear a route through Regenspasse for the 4th Armored Division to pass.

---

[7] Mauser was a German Arms manufacturer. They made bolt action rifles for the German army in WWII

**More surrender pictures of the
Eleventh Panzer Division.**

MORE COMBAT AFTER SURRENDER

The 3rd Battalion approached a small town situated in a shallow valley at the bottom of some gently rolling hills. We were spread out between some 4th armored tanks when word reached us that the SS troops were prepared to fight to the death. We laughed and continued advancing forward to the town. We had heard threats before. As we approached the town we spread ourselves between the tanks. The vaunted SS troops left from the other side of the town. (SS is the abbreviation for *Schutzstaffel*, German for "Protective Echelon".) This proved to me what cowards they really were. We entered the town walking down both sides of the main street. There was no resistance. I decided to test out my .30 caliber carbine by aiming and firing at some second story flower pots with only my right arm and hand. Three flower pots in one window confirmed my shooting ability. The street deadened at a cross street with a large stucco pink wall facing toward us. A picture of Hitler's face staring back at us brought a fusillade of fire from troops on both sides of the street. Of course Hitler's picture disintegrated into bits and pieces. Boy, was that a lot of fun!

We were moving forward now at a rather rapid pace, but eventually settled down for the night at a small farmhouse I was bunking down in the house along with a sergeant and a few other soldiers when the Second Lieutenant said, "Sabetay, take this message to the machine gun nest." I asked, "Where is it?" "Go in that direction." He indicated in what direction I was to go by gesturing toward the perimeter of our defense. I trotted off in the general direction he had indicated and looked for the machine gun nest. Dusk was rapidly setting in and I missed the machine gun nest. I continued in the direction indicated with my carbine ready to shoot when I came to a huge barn. The barn doors were open with nothing but blackness streaming out from the interior.

Entering the barn I heard voices in Czech, French, and other languages. There were lots of hands patting me on the back. Obviously, these people were quite happy to see an American GI. "Yeah, yeah," I answered. I slowly turned around and started walking back toward our lines. Now I had to think my way out of this one because that Second Lieutenant was waiting for my answer. I had a real dilemma on my hands. I realized that there was a machine gun nest out there somewhere. It was hard to see in the dark but at least I had the light of the moon. I shouldered my rifle and decided to approach as an unsuspecting enemy soldier. I could feel hundreds of eyes on my back as I slowly walked toward the lines. "Sabetay, is that you?" someone called. "Yes it's me!" I answered. "Thank God!" he said, "It was all I could do to keep this guy from firing on you. He had you dead in his sights and was a second away from shooting you when I convinced him not to fire." "How did you know it was me?" I rejoiced. "I recognized your walk," he said. I owe that soldier my life. There seemed to me to be an extra ordinate amount of miracles coming my way. All I could feel was gratitude.

I reported back after my strange encounter. I don't remember the outcome of the displaced persons who were in the barns. I did hope that they would have a peaceful and happy ending.

The next day we were loaded into trucks and tanks of the 4th Armored and toured victoriously through Czechoslovakia's countryside. A few stray German soldiers approached our column and attempted to surrender. A gunner operating a 30 caliber machine gun on one of the trucks opened fire and cut them down. It was a needless murder and I felt revulsion for the guy who did it. I remember now that I had another one of my premonitions that this was going to happen. I remember feeling that way in Mainz, Germany when one of our American soldiers was shot, or rather murdered, by a German. There were malcontent soldiers on both sides. They just seemed to buck the established 'rules of engagement.'

General Patton's third army had spearheaded a drive across the center of Germany and was heading for Prague, Czechoslovakia. We could sense the end of hostilities since the surrender of the Elite 11th Panzer Division. All kinds of rumors were circulating about the end of the war.

A small Czech city, made up of 2-story stucco homes on a 2-lane street was occupied by I Company. Eight of us were in a second floor front bedroom. Seated in a circle on the floor, we made small talk about souvenirs. Right then and there a fellow soldier by the name of Gissinger, who was seated directly across from me, pointed a .22 caliber derringer at me. "Point that gun somewhere else," I told him. "Why?" He replied, "It isn't loaded." "Well, this carbine is." I retorted as I swung the muzzle straight toward his middle. "Aim that gun at the ceiling and pull the trigger and see if it is loaded." He dutifully raised the automatic pistol and a loud noise preceded a shower of falling plaster. Nothing more was said after that incident.

Later we walked downstairs and ambled into the alley behind the house. Ivey ran toward us with a sling full of bazooka shells and a bazooka in his other hand. "Where are you going, Ivey?" I shouted. "Follow me," he said. We ran up to the second floor of a house with a bedroom overlooking the front street. He laid on his stomach, peering out a window. "There is a small German column there." "Load me!!" he yelled. Lying next to him, I took a shell and placed it into the tube, spun the wire to make an electrical connection, tapped him on the helmet to let him know it was armed. He fired and said, "I missed! Load me again!" I loaded a second shell, tapped him on the helmet, and he fired again. "Missed, damn it! Load it again!" Just then a German Panzerfurst (anti-tank weapon) flew through the window over our heads and hit the ceiling behind us. "Load!" he shouted. I loaded the bazooka again. Ivey aimed, fired, and shouted, "I got him! Let's get the hell out of here!"

There were rumors that there were German soldiers holed up in a 3-story stucco house. A group of us checked it out and found it to be false. The comment by one sergeant was that the war was almost over. We all felt like we did not want to risk our necks again, but nothing was official and there was no Cease Fire yet. We were all weary and drained. We just wanted everything to be over and soon.

We met up with the Russians in Czechoslovakia. We were on the outskirts of a small town on a narrow two-lane road. It was mud covered from the misty rain that fell on the open countryside. The Russians were a dour, non-smiling lot. Their uniforms were nondescript, brown, and dirty. They were all in a few trucks with an accompanying tank. After meeting them, we returned to our company.

PEACE DECLARED

We had taken over an apartment that was located over a cognac distillery. The two -story building was not that large, about 60 by 60 feet square. The apartment had a veranda on the front of the building with some nice looking canvas chairs.

PEACE WAS NOW DECLARED! Victory in Europe was now a reality. The German high command signed an unconditional surrender of all land, sea, and air forces to the American Expeditionary Forces. They also surrendered to the Russian High Command. This happened on May 7, 1945. It was a beautiful spring day! We were lounging on the veranda sunning ourselves when we received the news. What better place for this to have happened than over a cognac distillery!! Almost all the men proceeded to get drunk or happy. I chose to remain sober, to savor the peace and to reflect on all that had happened to me.

Pilsen, Czechoslovakia, was occupied by our troops. I was standing on the corner of a main intersection of the city. It was a wide boulevard bordered by Old World style buildings that were three, four, and five stories high. It was lovely city dressed in the old flavor of Europe. All of a sudden I saw two men walking rapidly past me from the left to the right carrying two Jewish Torahs. A torah is a sheepskin scroll rolled on two rollers that contain the five books of Moses written in Hebrew. These are also the first five books of the Bible. It was covered by an ornate cloth with two holes in the top for roller handles. What surprised me was how these two Jews and the torahs survived the German occupation, because the official policy of Nazi Germany was the extermination of all Jews.

Loaded onto eight two and a half ton GMC trucks, we headed back into Germany on the autobahn, a super highway that was built in the 1930's. The countryside reminded me of my home state of Ohio because of the similarity of the open fields and interwoven woods. The convoy came to a stop on the right side of the road. Lots of children came running to us, hoping that we had some candy or food. We handed out candy and K-rations. The convoy was preparing to leave when a Volkswagen car approached us at about sixty miles per hour. Just as it neared the back of our truck, a little ten-year-old boy got hit. He was hurled into the air, cart-wheeling and spinning. His face turned an ashen gray and he died instantly. The Volkswagen stopped. Two nurses in army uniforms and an army officer tried to see what they could do. At this point the convoy pulled out and I wondered how they were going to explain this tragedy to his German mother and family. We were all somber and silenced by this accident. A pall of gloom hung over us for quite a while as we left.

We passed several German Messerschmitt 109 pursuit planes parked along the side of the road. They had used the public road as a runway. I was sure wishing that I could get in one of those planes and fly it. The German Messerschmitt 109 (ME109) was a marvelous piece of machinery. German technology was sure ingenious and inventive. Germany had been clever and resourceful in building its war machine. None of Europe was ready for another war with Germany.

German Messerschmitt 109

ARMY OF OCCUPATION

The I Company pulled back, just inside the German border. We were bivouacked near a German concentration camp. A few survivors that looked like walking skeletons were being treated. This was the first time I had seen any concentration camp survivors. The name of that particular camp was Flossenberg. Later, we were assigned to a two-story former German barracks in Grafenwoehr. These four barracks were about 150 feet long and 50 feet wide with a peach-colored stucco exterior. They were lined up in a straight line some 25 feet apart at the ends. There was also a mess hall in a one story building which was 200 feet long with wood tables and benches. It was built over a 2-foot high crawl space. There was a parade ground in front and another open field off to the left.

I was assigned to a second story room with three other men. There were four bunks and wooden lockers for each of us. It also had wood plank floors and this room opened into a long hallway. The other side of the hallway had a huge empty room. It was used as an auditorium. We all settled into our new quarters now and were able to sleep on real beds instead of wet hard ground. Ah, peacetime! What luxury! The first day was totally free of any work.

Ivey and I were discussing what to do when I said, "Ivey, you know that German pistol with a bent barrel? Let's straighten it out." "How do you do that?" Ivey inquired. "Well, I've been thinking. There is a blow torch we can use. It's in the storeroom of the barracks." After we secured the blowtorch and tools, we proceeded to heat the barrel until it was cherry red. Ivey hammered the barrel until it was straight on an anvil. He held it up with a pair of tongs and sighted down the barrel. "It looks straight." "How do you temper it?" "That's easy," I replied. "All we have to do is quench it in the bucket of oil." Ivey plunged the barrel into oil and lifted the hissing barrel out. After it cooled, we assembled the pistol. All that remained was to test-fire it. "Gee, I don't know. Do you want to test fire it, Ivey?" "Bud, maybe it will blow up?" After due consideration, neither of us was willing to risk our lives on our handiwork. It was fun working on it anyway.

There was a radio in the Panther tank out back but it had a section missing. I knew there were some replacement parts in the store room. Picking up the parts, we carried them to the German tank, climbed in the turret, and settled down to assemble them. Telefunken[8] radios were made up of modular blocks, and, all we had to do was plug them in. The radio was switched on. A large calibrated dial back lighted by a yellow light shined brightly, and we were in business. Picking up the mike and depressing the button, I intoned, "Achtung, achtung, achtung!" The English translation for this is, "Attention, Attention, Attention!" Releasing the button, I waited for a reply. Switching channels and repeating the call did not succeed in my getting any response. "The war must truly be over," I thought.

Bud with Luger

I Company soldier with Luger in Pressath, Germany June 6, 1945

Tiring of the game, Ivey said, "Bud, there is a German small-tracked reconnaissance vehicle in the field near our barracks." After a short walk, we came upon the vehicle. Ivey climbed into the cockpit and started the engine. By grasping two sticks and flooring the accelerator, the vehicle moved very quickly. He guided

---

[8] Telefunkun was a German radio and microphone company dating back to 1903

it by pushing and pulling two sticks; one stick was for the right, and one was for the left. Circling around in a big arc he braked to a stop beside me. "Hop on the deck behind me and I will take you for a ride, Bud." I pulled myself up behind the cockpit and hooked my fingers over the edge of the deck. Ivey put the vehicle into gear and we roared off into the woods. For an hour, Ivey drove the vehicle through the woods and open spaces, dodging trees and other debris. Finally after an hour we came to a stop. The hood behind me had two flat doors covering the engine. The doors were cherry red with heat. The motor continued to idle without a miss. "Ivey, how the hell can that engine continue to run cherry red hot?" "I don't know," said Ivey. "They must have some technology we don't." "Look at the bogey wheel on the left side, it's bent up," I pointed out to Ivey. "I hit a root a mile back," Ivey replied. This was a unique track vehicle. I had never seen anything like it before. It was about 11 feet long with a deck behind the cockpit. The engine was in the back of the vehicle.

Returning to the barracks, we cleaned up and headed to the mess hall for supper. A pool of money was donated and German women were hired to cook and clean the mess hall for us. We got some German 12% beer in barrels so after the supper hour, the mess hall turned into a beer hall and entertainment center. That evening, I returned to the mess hall and purchased two steins of beer for ten cents. I sat down to relax and started to talk with a soldier who sat across from me. I asked him what he was drinking because he was obviously quite inebriated. He said, "I've been drinking anti-freeze!" He proceeded to brag about his exploits that he could drink anything. "Anti-freeze is a deadly poison," I said. My warning fell on deaf ears. Later on, an army ambulance took him to a hospital but the ambulance had a flat tire while on the way and the soldier died. After this incident, life soon changed, and army discipline was reinstated. There was drilling of the troops, posting of the guard, and training.

A group of us had a brief respite and left for the woods where we practiced target shooting. I had acquired two Luger pistols; a 1912 model (through bartering) and a 1943 model. I took the 1912 model with me and left the other in my unlocked locker. In the woods, I test-fired the pistol and found it to be a very accurate and reliable weapon. Upon returning to the barracks I found my locker had been ransacked and my 1943 Luger was missing. The following morning, the tall sergeant who had ordered me to cross No Man's Land in the grape vineyard to bring in the lost squad, stopped by to tell me he had taken the gun. "I needed the money," he said defiantly. "I sold it for $75." He was nothing but a thief in my eyes. This guy was extremely arrogant and a smart ass. To say the least, his character was lacking. Shortly after that, he shipped out to the United States and I could not pursue the matter any more.

Our company was about to guard an ammunition dump of gas shells. The German gas shells were stored in a forest with large open spaces. The shells were stacked in pyramids about twenty wide at the base and coming to a peak of seven feet. The third squad was assigned to a spot some 75 yards away from one pile of shells. There were literally thousands of gas shells stacked throughout the forest. We built a fire and set up camp with men posted to take turns guarding the artillery shells.

The next morning, two of us not on guard duty decided to do a little exploring and go hunting for some fun. A small creek ran parallel with the forest. Heading out toward the creek, about 50 yards in front of us, a large rabbit darted away. Both of us fired at the rabbit. My bullet hit the rabbit in the hollow between and above his eyes. The rabbit thrashed around on the ground, so I pumped three more quick shots at the rabbit, missing him completely. I picked up the rabbit by the ears after it stopped moving. We crossed the creek in a shallow spot and continued to travel. A flock of seagulls flew above us. Both of us fired and my cohort's bullet hit a sea gull, which fluttered down and landed in the creek, obviously in much distress. I felt badly for the bird and that we had fired at the flock. Walking away from the creek, we came to a plowed field with a furrow running crossways. A large brown rabbit forty yards from us ran out a long furrow. Both of us fired several shots, but mine missed. My buddy's bullet struck home and rolled the rabbit over several times. He picked up his rabbit by the large ears and carted it with us. "That was pretty good shooting on my part," my buddy bragged.

Heading back toward the woods, we approached a small German farm. "Do you suppose these people could use some meat?" I asked. "Let's see what happens," he replied. Rapping on the door, a middle aged man and woman appeared. Holding up the two hares by the ears, we indicated that we wanted to make a trade for them. We wanted some coffee but settled for chicory, a coffee replacement. It was better than we expected.

The next morning after a K-ration breakfast, we noticed two German girls, bent over some bushes. At the same time they made some sweeping motions with their arms. Two of us approached the girls and observed they had small wooden scoops with wire teeth on one end. They were scooping blueberries from the bushes. We weren't supposed to fraternize with the Germans, but this rule was not too closely followed. These were German farm girls who had evidently been doing this a long time before we arrived to guard the ammunition dump.

Two of us were walking toward a single lane road through the forest. A jeep with two GI's and two German girls approached us going about thirty miles per hour. As the jeep passed by, a gust of wind blew the long wavy hair of one of the girls. As her hair blew upward, I noticed that she was bald on the back of her scalp. Obviously, she had lice. The G.I.s were in for a rude awakening, I thought. Guaranteed!

The fourth day we were sitting around the camp when we noticed smoke rising in thick black clouds about 300 yards away. "My God, the ammunition dump is on fire!" one guy hollered. I grabbed my gas mask when one guy exclaimed, "Wait a minute! The wind is blowing away from us." Several guys didn't have a gas mask, because they had thrown theirs away when they became too cumbersome to carry! Because the wind was favorable to us we did not need our gas masks. Word reached us that an entire field hospital was being flown in. This could have been absolutely disastrous for the hospital. The fire eventually burned itself out and did not spread to the other stacks of shells. Thank God there were no casualties.

Later I had the chance to take a closer look at the woods where the fire had been. Only blackened stems of trees and earth were left in a square of approximately 150 yards on each side. A remark was made that nothing would grow in this area for 20 years. These gas artillery shells contained a form of mustard gas and other gasses. The only reason that they were not used was because we Americans also had them. Although both sides had these gasses, there was an unwritten law that neither side would use them.

Back in the barracks in Grafenwoehr, things returned to normal. I drew guard duty, protecting a German motor pool. The shelter for German vehicles was a long, low pole building with a sloping roof with an opening on the high end. Herman Goering had a huge open touring car called a Hortch, with half doors that opened in the back. I proceeded to sit in the front seat and imagined that I was riding through towns and the countryside.

The next guard duty that I drew was for the protection of the perimeter of the camp. By a chance encounter, I ran into Ivey. He was now a Second Lieutenant with Headquarters. I sure was happy for him. Ivey had made a battlefield commission! It certainly didn't hurt him that he was a former baseball player. That gave him points with the General who loved baseball. "Anything I can do for you Bud?" "Yes," I replied. "I'm going on guard duty this evening," I added. "Hmm, guard duty… aye?" That evening, right before I was to assume my responsibilities, the First Sergeant said, "Sabetay, you'll be acting Sergeant of the guard." That night proved uneventful; and it was a nice not to have to walk my post in a military manner. Previously I turned down a staff sergeant promotion from Reams, because the previous eight staff sergeants were either killed or wounded. Now I was a sergeant.

My assigned duty was to take two jeeps and patrol a perimeter of 320 miles. That was an awful lot of territory to cover in one day. Eight men in two jeeps were supposed to scare the German populace. These were direct orders from Headquarters. The army needed for them to have a healthy respect for us as the victors, and as the Army of Occupation. We didn't need any more guns fired at us. I put four men to one jeep and proceeded to take an American-German interpreter with me in the other jeep. I covered 160 miles with my crew, and the other group covered the other 160 miles of the perimeter. The first village was 20 miles away. We singled out a long house on the outskirts of a village. One of our G.I.s pounded on the door with the butt of his rifle. Then the interpreter snarled in a loud voice to open the door! An elderly German couple answered the door immediately, and asked what we wanted. "Orders to search your house," the German-speaking G.I. shouted! We checked the house but nothing of any adverse nature was found. Our interpreter frightened the German couple by telling them that this was no small matter. He knew that they would spread the news throughout the village.

In the next village we repeated the same scenario. One village produced an American Garand rifle with an exploded German bullet frozen in the chamber because the gun was a 30 caliber, and the bullet was a German 31 caliber. By now the scare tactics were employed in full. Our interpreter frightened the German couple by telling them that this was no small matter. We left it like that and arrived home around dusk.

My debriefing went fine until one of my men brought in the rifle with the frozen chamber. "Why wasn't this rifle inventoried?" demanded the interrogating officer. "I was about to do that," I answered. This was not a good situation that I found myself in mainly because of the way that it was presented. However, the subject was dropped after I explained that I was distracted and just got out of the jeep without it. I think what probably happened was, a German soldier picked up the Garand rifle as a trophy of war and a kid probably put a German bullet in it.

At 2:00 in the morning the platoon was rousted out of bed and assembled into the empty room across the hallway. We all were searched, but there was no explanation given as to why we were being searched. The next morning we found out that the other jeep that I sent out had searched the Herman Goering[9] Castle. Mrs. Goering had evidently called headquarters and told them that a jeep full of our men had robbed her. Days later I was offered a large yellow diamond for $100. I

---

[9] Herman Goering was second in command of he Nazi party, only next to Hitler himself. He founded the Gestapo (secret police) in 1933. He held the title of Reichsmarschall, making him senior to all other Wehrmacht commanders. He was also the commander in charge of the Liuftwaffe (German Air Force). After WWII, Goering was sentenced to death at the Nuremberg trials. He committed suicide by taking cyanide the night before his scheduled execution. He was also an abysmal morphine addict.

refused because I did not want to be party to a jewelry heist. It was puzzling to me as to where these men could have hidden the jewels until I found out that during the room search, the soldiers stood on some loose floorboards that concealed the jewels.

A few days later, as a Sargent, I was assigned ten men to occupy the town of Neustadt, which means "new town" in the German language. The town was anything but new. The Germans gave many towns this name. Neustadt was about 20 miles from Grafenwoehr. The town had a population of 1200 people. The mayor's house was an imposing two-story white stucco building. It was located north of town on the east side of the road.

We established our quarters on the second floor of the mayor's house. My first job was to set up a guard post on the main thorough fare about 100 feet west of the intersection. Every two hours two men were posted at the guard. An agreement was made with the mayor's wife to cook for all of us. We attained that arrangement by exchanging C-rations with her. Scavengers were sent out to barter for eggs and other food. Things worked out rather well for us, and we ate heartily

One evening, I was touring the town when, I came upon a lieutenant who was out of his area. I pretended not to see him. He was fraternizing with one of the German girls. He knew that this was forbidden but he was there anyway. It would have served no real useful purpose to turn him in at this point of the war.

Another day as a sergeant, I inspected the guard post and witnessed a guard allowing a ten-year-old boy to hold his rifle. I became livid, grabbed the rifle from the boy, and shoved it back into the guard's hands. "You hand a loaded rifle to a kid?" I admonished him after shoving the kid away. "Where is your brain? You hold that rifle in a military manner and you'd better not be caught doing anything stupid like that again!" I admonished.

A local washerwoman took it upon herself to report to me anything that happened in the community. She had been so brainwashed by the Nazi's that she would tattle on any and all adults. In Nazi Germany, the children were taught to tell on their parents and the adults were told to inform on each other. Her loyalty just

141

changed from Germans in charge, to Americans in charge. She was so used to a police state that she could not differentiate between good and evil. Consequently, I had unsolicited information on what went on around the town.

We kept getting reports that an S.S. soldier was about to return home. I contacted the O.S.S.[10] and they directed me to pick him up and hold him until they got there. S.S. soldiers were not being liberated at that time. I took a strong 6 foot 2 inch tall North Carolina soldier with me. This soldier had good manners and an affable personality. Together we walked to the T intersection, and then turned left and went to the last house on the right side of the street. Rapping on the door, a slightly wounded soldier, with balding hair, came to the door. We took him into custody and returned.

The O.S.S. officers arrived and took the German into a private room on the second floor. They interrogated him for two hours. Finally they just let him go. One of the O.S.S. officers came out to talk with me. He was Jewish, about 30 years old, very tall, and a little heavy Feeling a familiar spirit with me he began to fill me in on the real story. "This German had no tattoos, so he isn't an S.S. soldier. He blows like the wind blows. When you talk to him he agrees with everything that you say. If you change directions on him he goes along with you. This has turned out to be a false alarm," he said. We got the real story later. An American medic left over from the prior contingent had been shacking up with the German's wife. She fell in love with the American medic and wanted to get rid of her husband so that she could continue her tryst.

As a staff sergeant in charge of the occupation, a young woman came to ask me permission to visit her sister in the next town. I questioned her to some extent about what she did and about other things that pertained to her life. Finally, I was satisfied with her answers and her demeanor and wrote her the pass. A physician, who lived about two houses away from the mayor's house, wanted to play chess with me. He had heard that I knew how to play. Unfortunately, we never did get

---

[10] O.S.S. is the Office of Strategic Services. It was a U.S. intelligence agency that was formed during WWII. It was the predecessor to the C.I.A.

together for a good game. Lots of little interesting occurrences happened in that small town.

There was a young good-looking German boy, about 16 years old, with blonde hair, and blue eyes, and about 5 feet 10 inches tall. He lived right next door to the mayor. It was my duty to inspect all of the houses around us. He sprung to attention with his right arm outstretched in a Hitler salute. This happened in a fraction of a second before he gained his composure and realized who I was. He obviously was a product of Hitler. I should have reported him but never did. I thought at the time that the poor youth had been brainwashed and just did not know any better. I was hoping that my mercy on him would win him over to the greatness of freedom of thought without fear.

I was in charge of guard duty 24 hours a day for seven consecutive days. To make this work I set up a system in which two guards were assigned to each post. When their shift was over, one of the guards woke up the next shift. When the two fresh guards came on duty the previous guard was dismissed. Overall there were few problems on my periodic checks.

A few days later an officer showed up and called a meeting in our quarters. He wanted to know who was on guard at two o'clock that morning.

"Why?" I asked.

He answered, "Two men were found sleeping on guard duty."

"Who reported this?"

"There was a report in the suggestion box and it was checked out by the First Sergeant," the reply came.

I stalled as long as I could, then finally the two guilty G.I.s came forward and confessed. The officer read the riot act to us. He told the two that during wartime the penalty for sleeping on guard duty was execution by firing squad. He emphasized that they were to never let this happen again and he would take care of it.

Later on I learned that the First Sergeant was the one who, while quite drunk, rode with a jeep driver, and checked the guard post. When he found the sleeping guards, he should have been a man and informed me about the problem so I could take care of it instead of putting a report in a suggestion box. How low can you get?

The next day we returned to Grafenwoehr. Army training was again instituted. It was my job to drill the platoon. After all that drilling, the day came to a welcome end. I met up with a fellow sergeant who was in his early twenties. We decided to go to town and have some fun. Fraternization with the Germans was forbidden. However, we decided that we had enough boredom and that we needed a change of scenery. Skirting the outposts and patrols, we made our way to Grafenwoehr. It was a small nondescript town with ordinary-looking houses lining a narrow street with a small bar at the end.

We entered the bar and picked a couple of stools next to a group of elderly German workmen. We ordered a couple of beers and I noticed that mine was extra foamy. However, I noticed the rim of my stein was sticky. I drank the beer anyway. The bartender was a heavy middle-aged man with graying hair, a scowl on his face, and a personality to match it. We felt rather unwelcomed by this guy, so we decided to go back to the base by the same way that we came. Even though it wasn't a good sojourn, it gave us a chance to use our skills at being elusive.

A few days later I awoke with a strange metal taste in my mouth. On sick call, the physician in charge told me that I had trench mouth. "What do I do?' I asked the doctor. "Rinse your mouth with salt water until it goes away." He responded. After several days of using salt water rinses, my mouth returned to normal. I am convinced my trench mouth came from drinking that beer.

PARIS

I finally wrangled a pass to Paris and caught a ride. I don't remember the dates but it was summer and the weather was gorgeous. Before going, a soldier gave me a carton of German cigarettes and asked me to sell them for him. He also said that we could split the money. I protested, "German cigarettes are not in as much demand as American cigarettes." He assured me that they were in demand and I took them with me.

My first day in Paris, I was walking along a wide boulevard. A gendarme stopped me and asked, "How much for the cigarettes?" "You're kidding?" I said. "No monsieur," he answered in broken English. "Is it Okay? Can I buy the cigarettes?" Finally I made the deal for ten dollars' worth of French francs. At that time it struck me strangely that a French policeman would buy black market cigarettes. There were shortages of everything during and after the war.

My hotel was located some distance from the heart of the city. I don't remember the name of it now. The only thing I remember about the hotel was the way that they prepared the food. I had Spam in every way imaginable. They evidently obtained the canned wonder from the American army. The hotel room was sparsely furnished with a bed, a chair, a bidet, and a toilet. The room was large with white walls and a high ceiling. I never saw a bidet before and upon learning what it was for, I became somewhat amused.

As I was investigating Paris, I had fun traveling through the subways and thoroughfares. I finally stumbled on a small jewelry store and watch repair shop on the outskirts of town. I took in my Omega 15-jewel watch to have the twisted hands and crystal replaced. I had purchased the watch from my roommate but he had broken it in a fight. That evening I left the hotel to see the sights of Paris. Wandering through the streets, I noticed a crowd of civilians and soldiers lined up at a theater. It was the Folies Bergere! Upon entering the theater I noticed that there was standing room only. Nude showgirls stood like statues on the stage. The production was done in an artistic manner. That was my first time of experiencing anything like that form of entertainment.

Leaving the theater, a nearby café beckoned me to come in. It had the sound of soft music through the opened door. Inside the café was a gorgeous woman in a slinky red dress, sitting on a grand piano. She had a rather throaty sound to her voice as she sang torch songs. After I downed a few cognacs, I proceeded out onto the street to further savor the sights and sounds of the city.

Sauntering down a dimly lit street, a woman of slight build hurried past me. Emboldened by the cognac that I had consumed, I called, "Mademoiselle!" She slowed her walk so that I could walk by her side. One thing led to another and we ended up in a small sparsely furnished apartment that consisted of a combination living room, bedroom, kitchen, and bathroom. She offered me a drink of cognac and I accepted. She excused herself to freshen up a bit and to change her clothes. She emerged from the bathroom wearing a pink slip that ended halfway above her knees. She initially struck me as a very thin woman. She turned out to have an exquisitely formed body, with an attractive thin face, and brown hair. The slip concealed just enough to be a real turn-on. She proved to be quite adept at making love while still trying to keep everything very quiet: as it was late at night. In the morning it was an entirely different story with her. She demanded several hundred Francs in a loud demanding voice. No longer was being quiet in vogue. After paying her, she quieted down and we consulted a map of Paris so I could find my way back to my hotel. French Francs were not worth much on the exchange with the American dollar.

I returned to my hotel and wearily climbed the stairs, entered my room, fell into bed, and drifted off to sleep. That afternoon, I showered, shaved, and dressed. It felt so luxurious just to do normal things without a bunch of army guys in a barracks. Lunch in the hotel consisted of Spam, greens, and wine.

I took my own tour of Paris and saw the famous Notre Dame Cathedral. A tour guide told us that that the flying buttresses are all that support the walls. It was a magnificent cathedral. Unfortunately, I did not get to see the inside. Napoleon's tomb was situated in a round building with a circular pin and black marble wall. The catafalque containing Napoleon's body was constructed of several different layers of material with the outside encased in marble. In order to see the tomb, I had to peer over the wall and bow my head to see the catafalque below me. In retrospect that was one way to solicit a bow. After leaving the tomb, I observed several government buildings that were constructed during Louis the 14th's reign. The Palace of Justice and several other buildings were four to five stories high and constructed with limestone. These beauties were done in classic French styling and were at least 1000 feet long. They were breathtakingly beautiful.

There was an exhibition of V1 and V11 jet bombs and rockets that were used against London. Someone had cutaway their outward skin only to expose the intricate workings of the mechanisms propelling the bombs of death. Traveling west along the Seine River, I could see the Eiffel Tower with its tall spire arching into the blue sky. Under its base was a B-17 bomber on display. Although I only saw the Eiffel Tower from a distance, it impressed me as a magnificent structure. Continuing along the Seine River, I marveled at the artistic scenery of Paris. It was a pure delight to see such beauty.

It was late at night now after my tour and I found myself walking down a dark two-lane street. Again I was trying to find my hotel. The sidewalks butted into the sides of the buildings on both sides of the street. Needless to say, these were narrow streets very dark and eerie. I decided to walk down the center of the street for safety reasons. There were lots of black alleys emptying into this street. There were no streetlights, only starlight. Tales of at least one dead soldier floating down the Seine River every night tempered my enthusiasm. It just wasn't a good idea to walk past dark alleys. Walking rapidly down the street, I was surprised to see another person in white appear from a side street on my right. He wore a chef's hat, a white coat, and white pants. My logical explanation was that he was a chef. Staring hard at him, I noticed that he was about 5 feet 10 inches tall and somewhat portly. "Good evening," he greeted me jovially in flawless English. Returning the greeting, I asked him the way to my hotel. He explained to me that my hotel was a few blocks away and offered to walk part of the way with me to set me in the right direction.

We struck up a conversation and I learned that we had something in common. We were both Jewish. He told me that he had survived the war in Paris as a chef. We parted after a few blocks and I reflected on what an odd happenstance that was.

MY COUSIN ALEX

I returned to Grafenwoehr and again was immersed in training. One day a line of trucks passed through and was stopped momentarily. I recognized one of the drivers of a 773rd field artillery truck. I approached the truck and struck up a conversation with him. I inquired as to what happened to the 773rd field artillery. "After you left," he said, "over half of the outfit was lost in the Battle of the Bulge." He couldn't help but notice my sergeant stripes and I couldn't help reflecting what a bitter hand fate had dealt the 773rd. Fate, on the other hand, had dealt a good hand to me when I drew that third straw way back when.

Rumors were flying that we were going back to the states and then on to fight the Japanese. However, before that happened we heard about some super bomb that was dropped on Hiroshima in Japan. Three days later another bomb was dropped on Nagasaki, Japan. It was beyond the realm of understanding how two bombs could obliterate two whole cities. On August 15th V.J. (Victory Over Japan) was declared and the war was over. Really over!

Now there was a really different feeling and the troops were no longer worried about the future. Word came down that I was to go to corps headquarters in Regensburg. I was to be briefed on the benefits that were due to the men who would be honorably discharged. Before I left, one sergeant told me that he and another sergeant had been approached first for this assignment. His words did not hurt my feelings because I looked forward to any new experience that I could get. And, to take the cake, my cousin, Alex Sunshine, was in core headquarters in Regensburg.

The next morning I left on a truck for Regensburg. For some reason the truck was routed through Nuremburg to Regensburg. Upon reaching Nuremburg some two hours later, I was astounded by the sight that greeted me. Rubble was piled four feet high as far as the eye could see. We turned southeast and continued another 65 miles to Regensburg. I arrived about three o'clock in the afternoon. I was impressed by the differences in the two cities. The buildings were still intact, and there was very little devastation noticeable.

I was assigned to a second story barracks where I settled in. I found a shower, cleaned up, and changed my clothes just in time for dinner. Dinner in corps headquarters didn't consist of spaghetti or macaroni as it did in division companies. We had steak prepared any way that we wanted. The further up you climbed the ladder to command headquarters, the better the food was.

That evening I got in touch with my cousin, Alex. Boy, was I ever glad to see him. He was awfully glad to see me too. He was very good to me as a kid, and I truly realized, what a breath of fresh air he was. We hugged and I was all smiles. Alex was about 6 feet 2 inches tall, and weighed in at about two hundred pounds. He had dark straight brown hair and a wide ready smile. Alex had escaped from Nazi governed Austria in 1938 and eventually reached the states where he stayed with my grandparents on Orchard Avenue in Barberton, Ohio. He came to the US having graduated from high school at the age of sixteen. The education he received in Europe was equivalent to a college education here in the States.

Since he spoke fluent German, he was assigned to the intelligence department in corps headquarters. That night Alex took me to the Non Com Club (Non-Commissioned Club) for some fun. It was in a large building with a bar on one side of the room. Wooden tables and chairs filled the rest of the room. "Bud," Alex said, "Here is a ration book for drinks. I have some business in town. Enjoy yourself and I'll be back in a few hours." Upon examination of the book, I saw that there were coupons for all sorts of drinks including Tom Collins, Bloody Marys, and Scotch and Soda. You name it and it was there. Since I was not one to let a golden opportunity go to waste, I attempted to drink my way through the book. What a way to relax. After several mixed drinks, I was feeling pretty happy. A couple of sergeants who were feeling good also, commenced to relay their war stories. We were having a good time trying to outdo each other with our stories. The more we drank the louder the conversation got. A fellow soldier offered me a canteen cup of rum. By this time I had already drunk my way through half of the ration book. He would take a sip and then I would take a sip. This went on for some time. We were commiserating with each other in a drunken stupor. The thing that I do remember was that there was a little sober black box of memory recording everything in my mind that night.

Alex finally arrived after a few hours, with a bottle of cognac. It appeared that was the business at hand for the night. I apologized for using up half of his coupon book. Alex didn't mind at all. By then we were so drunk that we were slurring our speech. I was starting to feel sick to my stomach and dizzy. Excusing myself, I staggered to the barracks and headed for the latrine. I grasped the side of the toilet bowl and heaved until my gut was empty and green bile appeared.

After dry heaving for a while my dizziness subsided and I headed for my bunk to sack out. Morning came too quickly. After all, I had classes to attend. Too sick to eat breakfast, I headed for the bus stop. A bus arrived and I proceeded to board it. I took two steps up, took one look at the bus driver, and got back off. I was so nauseated that I decided to walk to town for my classes. I was walking toward town when two military policemen stopped me and tried to get me to go to the hospital. "Soldier, you are green around the gills," one of them said. "I know. I tied one on last night," I replied. I finally convinced them to let me continue on. I walked about two more blocks and an M.P. captain stopped me. "Soldier, you look terrible, you are actually green. I'll take you to the hospital," he said to me. Again I managed to talk my way out of going to the hospital. Putting one step in front of the other steered me to a nondescript building one and a half miles to town where a meeting was in progress. There were about 20 officers and sergeants attending, with a captain who was conducting the seminar. My officer took one look at me and sent me back to sleep it off.

That evening dinner was served and things were back to normal. After three days of briefing I finally learned what we were entitled to upon discharge. The time went by quickly and it was time for me to go back to Grafenwoehr. I sure was glad to see my cousin, and I hated to leave him. I asked, "Alex is there any other way back other than by truck?" Alex replied, "Bud, there is a mail plane that leaves corps headquarters for Bayreuth and you can catch a truck from there back to Grafenwoehr." That suited me just fine. I always wanted to fly. Later that afternoon, Alex took me to a small airfield where a yellow Taylor craft sat idling. A Taylor craft was a small high wing monoplane with strut-supported wings, fixed landing gear, and a small underpowered engine. These planes were used for reconnaissance and directing artillery fire over enemy territory.

The pilot sat waiting for me impatiently. He was a lean young man in his late twenties with clean cut features and sandy hair. He indicated for me to climb into the rear seat beside a small sack of mail. I waved goodbye to Alex as the pilot revved up the engine and we taxied out for the take off. Turning into the wind the pilot pushed the throttle forward to gather speed and we were off. We were skimming over low lying mountains. The door on the side folded down from the top and was open to my knees. I could watch the scenery by slightly leaning out and looking down. Gusts of wind shook the plane and the pilot was not that happy because of the extra weight that I had added. Realizing the situation, I decided to make the best of it and prayed we would make it safely back. The only consolation that we both had was that I only weighed one hundred and forty pounds. Eventually we made it to Bayreuth, a sizeable town in northern Bavaria, and landed uneventfully.

DISCHARGE

The thing that seemed so odd upon returning to the base was that I wasn't called upon to inform the men of their discharge rights. When discharge time came I found out I needed five more points in order to be eligible. After racking my brain, I remembered that my finger was wounded by shrapnel in the Ardennes during the Battle of the Bulge. It had drawn blood and the shrapnel was still in my finger.

Armed with this evidence, I broached this subject with the company doctor. The Doctor examined me and I was awarded the Purple Heart. I got those five points that I needed which made me eligible for deployment to the good old USA.

Deployment was a time-consuming journey. It began with men eligible for discharge being separated from their friends. Then there came a long train trip to camps in France that were named after famous American cigarettes, like, Lucky Strikes, Camels, Chesterfields, and so on. Upon arrival at the Chesterfield Camp, we were assigned to circular tents, consisting of ten men per tent. There were several rows of tents neatly arrayed in straight lines with their entrances facing each other.

It was autumn and the weather was rather cool so there was a pot belly stove in the middle of each tent. Wood was used for fuel, and the stoves turned red with heat. It was either too hot or too cold, depending on where your cot was situated in the tent. The waiting began. Yes, it was the army as usual. "Hurry up and wait." Week after monotonous week went by, only broken up by passes to Paris, Brussels, or the French Riviera. I was never able to obtain a pass to Brussels or the French Riviera

Army blankets on a vacant cot were used for bartering in a nearby town by some of the men. You could get ten dollars for one of them. A wire fence became an obstacle that was put up to impede these trips to the town. After six years of war I could understand that the French people just wanted to be left alone. They wanted their country back in order to have some semblance of normality.

One evening, I again was assigned as Sergeant of the Guard. Men from my tent were assigned to be on guard duty. About two o'clock in the morning, one of the men on duty appeared in our tent to warm himself by the pot belly stove. "What are you doing?" I shouted. "I'm warming myself," he replied. "Get your ass back on guard duty!" I retorted in a commanding voice. He scampered out like a scared rabbit. The next morning he questioned me about my tough gruff attitude. I explained that I was still in charge and we were still in the army of occupation. He had a difficult time reconciling my ordinary demeanor with my commanding style.

GOING HOME

On my last pass to Paris, I scoured the city by subway from one end of it to another. I was looking for gifts for my mother, father, and sisters. Dad always smoked cigarettes, but would often smoke a pipe. This struck me as a nice gift to give him upon my return home. But there was no pipe to be found. Even the stores on the wide boulevards in the upscale part of Paris yielded nothing. Then I thought about the 8 X 45 binoculars I had and decided this was the best gift for my Dad. I continued to look for gifts for my mother and sisters. Finally in a large department store in another section of Paris I found the ideal gifts for them. I bought perfume for my mother and my twin sister, and a gold bracelet for my younger sister who had just turned sixteen.

Upon returning to the Chesterfield Camp, I learned we were going to the Port of Marseilles in southeastern France. On arrival there, we were assigned to the cruiser USS Savannah. Before boarding, every fifth soldier was searched for contraband. Climbing the gangplank was a welled up joyful feeling for me as I realized that I was really going home. The port was filled with other ships which were loading for the trip home.

My quarters were one deck down in the fan tail. Vertical piers of canvas bunks were stacked from the floor to just below the ceiling. My bunk was the third one up. After a few hours the ship moved out and we slowly left the port. Soon we were on the open seas and headed for the states. The air was cool and felt pleasant on my face as I stood on the deck.

The next day after mess, my size 750 binoculars came in handy. I walked to the bow of the deck and scanned the ocean ahead of the ship. Much to my surprise, a mine with spines and spikes was bobbing in the waves off the port bow. I gestured to the bridge and pointed to the mine. The ship immediately started to move in a wide arc around the mine. Shells were dropped from the ship to blow up the mine. Some of them fell short and some just missed the mark completely. Then, a marksman on the bridge, armed with a Garand rifle fired several rounds and hit the mark. The mine then proceeded to sink into the depths of the ocean. I found out that even though the war was over, there were plenty of booby traps out there.

There wasn't much to do except rest, trade stories, eat, and look forward to our arrival. But that was soon to change.

The USS Savannah was built in the year of 1939. Originally it was a slim, sleek ship, some 600 feet long. Along the way, she was altered by widening her amidships to accommodate anti-aircraft guns. This caused the ship to be top heavy and not very sea worthy. The Savannah was hit by a 500 pound bomb in the Mediterranean Sea. The bomb had exploded into the bowels of the ship and twisted the keel. The keel could not be straightened even though everything else was repaired. Since the keel is a main structural element of a ship, it would corkscrew through the water if it hit 22 knots.

In the mid afternoon, a cruiser paralleled our course at about 5000 yards out. It turned out to be the sister ship of the USS Savannah, the USS Augusta. The original skipper of the USS Augusta was now the skipper of the Savannah. The USS Augusta was passing us in mid ocean. Understandably, our skipper was not too happy with the sight of his old ship passing him. We were delayed by the mines and had standing orders to sink all of them.

That evening I climbed into my bunk, propped my hands behind my head, and listened to big band music emanating from a speaker mounted near the hatch. While dozing, I was suddenly jolted awake by a violent rolling sensation arising from the ship. I had to hang onto the bunk piers for dear life. The ship quickly righted it, but the stern rose out of the water, with its propellers spinning into the air. It finally hit the sea with a lurch.

My head jerked hard to one side. Big band music and static continued coming from the speaker as if nothing were happening. The stern gyrated around, slamming into and out of the water without letting up. The men hung onto their bunks wondering if they would survive the sea. The irony was not lost on us. We had all made it through some of the worst battles of the war. Toward the morning the sea quieted down. We were able to dress and get on deck, even though the middle of the ship was roped off.

Cold weather spray and mountainous waves at least 40 feet high came crashing onto the deck. A sailor filled us in on what happened. The cruiser rolled 42 degrees and righted itself during the height of the storm. The ship was not supposed to roll over more than 39 degrees on the inclinometer. Life boats on the top deck were smashed to splinters. The skipper's cabin was flooded with oil when a safety valve malfunctioned and a propeller shaft burned out. Bow plates sprung and leaked. Despite all of these shortcomings, the USS Savannah was able to limp home. The waves continued unabated throughout the next day. Troops were reduced to eating K-rations because no food could be served with the constant pitching and rolling of the ship. For some unknown reason, I never got sea sickness.

A lieutenant sent me on an errand to the bridge the next night to find the location of rain slickers for the men on watch. That particular day, the seas were much calmer. Upon entering the bridge, an oasis of calm struck me. Only a few men were on duty. They manned the wheel and the radar system which was displayed by a soft green light.

Having secured the information, I descended the ladders to the deck and delivered the information to the lieutenant. The following day, another storm was encountered and we again ate K-rations. Results from the two storms put the ship 400 miles off course. These storms finally ceased and we steamed on toward the east coast of the U.S.

Near the end of the trip, I learned about a big craps game that was taking place below the amidship deck. This game went on for two days before we arrived in New York. One soldier won twenty thousand dollars of gold-backed issued money. I can imagine the agony for some and the ecstasy for others that took place for all of those involved.

The port of New York was a welcomed sight for our homesick eyes to behold. The Statue of Liberty beckoned us as we sailed by it. We could hardly take all of it in. We were finally home. Wow, what a sight and feeling. My heart was ready to burst with pride and joy, just looking at the port of New York. To this day my; heart has a love for this country that, I believe, you can only acquire from seeing the opposite of real freedom.

FINALLY

As soon as we disembarked, we were hustled onto a train that was on its way to Indian Town Gap.[11] This was the first time that I ever rode on an electric train. As I gazed out the window, I noticed that the telephone poles were passing by in a blur. This was the fastest train ride I had ever experienced. It was sort of like those French subway trains.

We arrived at Indian Town Gap in the evening. We were assigned barracks upon arrival. The next morning after breakfast the discharge procedure started. A barrage of questions followed.

"Do you have any physical disabilities?"

"Yes, a piece of shrapnel in my left forefinger."

"Any other disabilities?"

"Yes, aggravated sinus trouble," I answered.

Everything was duly noted and we were briefed on the G.I. Bill of Rights. Our medical rights and our civil and educational rights were specified. We were given our Ruptured Duck pin (The Honorable Service Lapel Pin), and $200 mustering-out pay. Then we were warned not to accept any rides into town because there had been a rash of robberies.

I was discharged on December 2, 1945. I walked out the front doors of the Separation Center into a beautiful, sunny, winter morning. Two other discharged soldiers started to walk toward the bus stop with me when a big sedan pulled up beside us at the curb. "Hey soldiers, want a ride to town?" "Sure," answered one of the soldiers with me. "But they told us not to accept any rides," I said quietly. "What are you worried about?" one soldier asked. I speedily thought it over and

---

[11] Fort Indian Town Gap is a Pennsylvania army post. It was used for discharging soldiers in WWII. It is 23 miles northeast of Harrisburg, PA

concluded that anyone who would mess with the three of us would have to be crazy. These two army buddies were bigger than I was; and in shape to boot. We climbed into the back seat, with me in the middle.

The two in the front struck me as the characters in the newspaper comedy, "Mutt and Jeff." The man behind the wheel was a hulking individual with a bottle-brush mustache and a small brimmed hat on his head. His suit was a small brown checkered pattern. His buddy had a small pinched face with sandy hair. He wore a gray sports coat. Boy, I thought to myself, "These guys are a couple of really nefarious characters. As the car pulled away from the curb, the guy with the pinched face turned toward us and asked, "Do they give you mustering pay?" I smiled to myself and decided to play their little game.

"No" I answered. "They will send a check to us later."

"Get any souvenirs?" He asked

"Sure, I have it right here." I answered as I parted my Eisenhower jacket, to reveal a Luger pistol butt which was sticking out of my holster. I patted it with my right hand and said, "I know how to use it too." With that statement, he didn't ask any more questions and we had no worry of being robbed. What he didn't know was that the old German had made the shoulder holster so tight that I couldn't get the gun out with two hands in that position. I had no bullets for it either. Pulling up to the train station, we bid our hosts a goodbye and thanked them for the ride.

I phoned home to tell my family when to expect me. The Erie Lackawanna passenger train passed through Akron, Ohio, my hometown. Boarding the train I found a seat beside a beautiful young lady wearing a smart black business suit and a pill box hat. She sure was a sight for sore eyes. It sure felt good sitting next to a real full-blown American girl. We struck up a conversation and I filled her in on where I had been. She told me that she was on a business trip to Pittsburgh. Time quickly passed, and before long we were approaching her destination, she asked me if I would like to stop off in Pittsburgh. I seriously considered it, but decided that my family would be waiting for me and that I didn't want to disappoint them.

The rest of the trip was uneventful. I thought about coming home and looked forward to peacetime. The train finally pulled into the Akron depot, an old building with long stairways to the track. I disembarked, carrying my army gear and looked for friendly faces. There were very few people getting off and very few friendly faces to greet them. I looked around but it was to no avail. No one from my family was there. I felt terribly disappointed. I just couldn't understand it. With that situation, I hailed a cab and headed for home.

The cab turned left off Copley Road and stopped across the street from 523 Wildwood Avenue. I paid the cabbie and thought; "Perhaps I would have better luck this time." The front door was unlocked as it always was. I entered to find no one home. Carrying my duffle bag upstairs, I turned left and entered my room. It was just as I left it. I unpacked and stretched across the bed and decided to wait for the family. Had I known how this was going to turn out, I would have stayed in Pittsburgh. I thought about my last time home which was during furlough. The war had really seasoned me, and I wondered how I would react to things now. Would I be the same person or would I appear totally different to everyone. I was still Bud Sabetay, but I had sure been through a lot. At that moment, I decided to make the best of whatever life had in store for me.

Late in the afternoon, Mom came home. Elaine, my younger sister came home from school. Reva, married a month before I came home, was living in Boston. Dad came home from his partnership business, F&S Auto Wrecking. I tried to hide my depressing disappointment from them and I think that I was successful at it. However, I was still so very glad to be home.

I asked my sister and mother if they liked their gifts from Paris. Elaine's so-called gold bracelet turned green and was too small. The Parisian perfume stained their clothes. The binoculars that I had given dad were the best gift and he really appreciated them. I did not realize until that moment that Paris and all of Europe were so devoid of real authentic commodities. I had another pair of binoculars for Uncle Sam whom I dearly loved. We were all invited to his home the following night for dinner. Mr. Murphy, my next door neighbor, and my Dad took me out the second day. They wanted to relive my experiences, vicariously through me. I was not that forthcoming because I was a little shy and very private. We did end up reliving some of my experiences and all in all had a good time of it.

The next morning Dad came into my bedroom and touched my knee. I suddenly sprang up at him from a sound sleep, scaring him half to death. I guess I had more unwinding to do than I realized.

Before I end this story, I would like to relate an anecdote told to me as to how an insignificant event can influence one's life. These events can become a life or death matter in some cases.

I grew up with a boyhood friend by the name of D. A. Hardman. D.A. learned from me that my cousin from Austria, Alex Sunshine, had taught me how to play chess. He also wanted to learn the game in the worst way. So I asked Alex, "How about teaching my friend to play chess?" "Alright Bud." He said. We walked the mile from my grandfather's house on 580 Orchard Avenue in Barberton to where D.A. lived on Wesleyan Avenue. Alex taught D.A. well. In turn D. A. loved the game. We were both about 14 ½ years old at the time.

During the war, D.A. was captured as a P.O.W. by the Germans. A German guard befriended him because he could play chess. One day the guard told him the prisoners were going on a march. "D.A.," the German said, "When we come to a woods, I want you to slip away and escape." "Don't ask any questions. Do as I say." When they came to a wooded area, D.A. did as he was told. He found safety at a small German farm where he worked and survived until the end of the war. Many of those prisoners of war were outright murdered. Learning the game of chess had literally saved D.A.

A NOTE FROM THE AUTHOR

I often felt that the things that happened to me in the War prepared me to overcome any situation no matter how bad it was. These experiences help me to make the right decisions in civilian life. I want people to know what happened in those years. When I was young I didn't talk about it. As I got older I talked about it. Now I feel relief and am glad that I could share my experiences with you. I have had a good life, a good wife, and children. I hope you enjoyed my story.

Many of the things that had happened to me during my training I thought were bad for me. It turned out they were actually better for me, and predestined for me, so that I would make it out alive. I also feel that I became a better person for it.

I found out that we all have a purpose in this life. If we cooperate with our circumstances, and don't become bitter, our life will have meaning beyond our expectations. My goal was to become a pilot, but we lost an awful lot of our B17's, and the boys in them, in the bombings that occurred over Germany. I probably would have died a premature death, but the hand of destiny would have its way.

(Note from Editor: Robert Sabetay spoke at the Word War II - Korean War Roundtable. His speeches of November 2009 and March 2010 have been recorded and can be found at the University of Akron Archival Services. He was the fifth inductee into the Speakers Hall of Fame in March 2013.)